A SI DOG NAMED PAIGE

A REMARKABLE STORY ABOUT
A WONDERFUL HELPER FOR A
WOUNDED VETERAN

MITCHELL KRAUTANT

A Service Dog Named Paige
A REMARKABLE STORY ABOUT
A WONDERFUL HELPER FOR A WOUNDED VETERAN

Copyright© 2020 by Mitchell Krautant
All rights reserved. No part of this publication may be reproduced, distributed, or transmitted in any form or by any means, including photocopying, recording, or other electronic or mechanical methods, without the prior written permission of the publisher, except in the case of brief quotations embodied in critical reviews and certain other noncommercial uses permitted by copyright law.

For permission requests, write to the publisher, addressed "Attention: Permissions Coordinator," at the address below.

Ingram Content Group
One Ingram Blvd.
La Vergne, TN 37086
www.ingramspark.com

Printed in the United States of America

First Printing, 2020

ISBN 978-1-952740-20-6 (Hardback)
ISBN 978-1-952740-19-0 (Paperback)
ISBN 978-1-952740-18-3 (EPUB)

mkrautant.com
mitchellkrautant@gmail.com

TABLE OF CONTENTS

THE FIRST 2 YEARS AND 5 MONTHS OF HAVING A SERVICE DOG	5
MARCH 2017 CLASS FOR ME TO GET MY SERVICE DOG PAIGE	57
THE NEXT PERIOD WITH THE SERVICE DOG PAIGE	89
DAILY COMMANDS TO PAIGE	129
ANOTHER PERIOD OF TIME WITH PAIGE	155
QUESTIONS TO PAIGE ABOUT SCIENCE	197
PAIGE'S TRIP WITH SUNSHINEY	213
I FAILED MY TEST WITH PAIGE, HAD A CLASS ON HER, THEN RECOVERED	217
PAIGE'S HEALTH	233
DISEASES AND INFECTIOUS AGENTS	237
Biography of Mitchell Krautant	263

THE FIRST 2 YEARS AND 5 MONTHS OF HAVING A SERVICE DOG

INTRODUCTION: (I got her, my Service Dog, which was a female named Paige, in March 2017. I had put in for a grant for a Service Dog in 2015 and Canine Support Teams, the people who train Service Dogs and assign their owners, gave birth to Paige and trained her as a Service Dog for 2 years straight. Then, trained as a Service Dog, they put me through a 2-week course to learn about her and train her. I passed the course. This is a story about what it was like to have a Service Dog and what intelligent things she does for me. This chapter starts out in May 2017 and covers the next 2 years and 5 months of having her. Further chapters cover more. The next chapter is about what the March to March 2017 class was like to get her. Enjoy this reading! You'll like it, especially if you appreciate the character of Dogs!)

051517

I asked my phone to play a song about me and Paige.

"Sail" came on.

"This is how an Angel dies,

Blame it on my own sick pride,

Blame it on my ADD"

ADD stands for Attention Deficit Disorder. The summary of the song? Start writing again, because Paige is going to be helping with her Angelic Unicorn soul to help me accomplish them!

060117

I had to put Paige in the car for almost 10 hours to take her with me to see Krishna's brother, who is in the waiting line to get open-heart surgery.

She has been really good. The problem is that she is not eating her dog food, and it gave her diarrhea. Now she is eating left-over steak and bacon from the hotel room Service.

Ooooh! Let me see if this will automatically capitalize the term Service Dog...

It DID it DID! Hooray!

Paige was really good at the Cheesecake Factory last night. She was sitting in the only space available- in the aisle (the table was full of people) and I had to keep her tight next to the table so the waiting staff could move and serve. Paige did an excellent job, staying put the whole time and keeping her tail close in so nobody would step on it. She also kept rubbing her head on my hands, to get me to scratch her head. Very enjoyable and excellent Dog!

060617

While waiting in the front yard for Dial-a-Ride, laying on the grass against a tree with Paige's leash strapped to my belt, we ran into a problem. Across the street was a lady walking a tiny dog, and she called over to me asking if I was all right. Paige saw the little dog and started bolting after it! I had to grab the handle on her vest and cry out "leave it! Leave it!" She pulled me so hard that it knocked my book into the parking spot and knocked my walker sideways into the street. Very troubling.

We are outside of Creme de la Creme Bakery waiting to get picked up. She'll arrive soon, so I am going to put the phone away now.

060717

I took Paige to Red Robin for lunch. The burger was deeeelicious, and so was the appetizer and French fries! Paige was snacking on leftovers (I had forgotten her treats) and wanted more, more, more! She is an excellent dog. Sometimes I feel bad for her. I am so forgetful about the treats!

080517

Paige is coming up and getting pet a lot lately. I think she is getting it in mind that I am a nice person who likes to pet her, so she stays really quiet and softly lifts her head up in a way that she would hold it if it was being pet. A Very intelligent Dog! Peaceful and kind, too! Well, for the most part. She jumped into Krishna's room today and tried to sic Sunshiney, our cat. Krishna had to grab her and keep screaming "no! no!" until I came in and grabbed her by the collar and led her out. She followed, but man, she was feisty! I didn't hurt her or anything, but she really wanted to hurt that cat. That makes me worry. Not so much so that we locked her out of the room. We left the door open for her to come back in because we want her to get used to Sunshine, so we are going to be working with her.

080617

I decided tonight to spend a late night learning about physics and writing on the computer, and Paige began to look at me with her head raised up and her eyes all big, because she is interested in me staying awake and getting back on the program of writing.

I am going to write a lot of ideas about science up. The goal is to make ideas related to science so extreme that one can take the ideas and put the experiments to work and actually accomplish what the theory is. I am going to be trying to do for science what students of 9 years of Quantum Theory are able to do, with only reading and 1 year of college behind it. If I pull it off, it will be amazing. My IQ test in Force Recon was a 98 out of 100 questions right, which made me smarter than every person there in that company that I was told about. That is the IQ of Albert Einstein. Or near it. So, I must find a way to put these ideas down on paper in a good way for reading.

So how does Paige play into that? I am going to be reading to her some of what I write down as I write it, and I am going to be reading to her parts of the books I am reading, and I will be taking knowledge from her reaction to what I say to what I should put in regards to the theories. Paige is an extremely smart Dog, so I know, I just know, that she will understand the concepts of science I put before her and know that she will help me put it forth in miraculous terms.

Of note, Krishna thinks that Paige looks like a Unicorn (and so do I), so the other day she bought for me a Unicorn doll that looks just like her! Amazing!

080717

Paige is sitting on my bed, laying down and licking my foot. A delightful Dog she is!

081617

Paige is acting remarkably friendly today. A woman came by in the coffee shop to pet her and Paige was nice and plentiful with it. I am certain that she can sense what a person who is petting her or coming around us is thinking, and if they are thinking anything related to violent action against her or I, she barks at them and gets ready to sick them! A great dog!

Let me talk a little bit about writing. There is an element of the mind that has ideas about things that correlates to the actual presentation of those said events. How that works I have no idea. How can I have the idea that I could talk about martial arts, in a Buddhist temple, by priests, who are seeking with their minds the answers to the mysteries of the universe, like death? Each of those things seems to require a picture in the mind of them happening, but I didn't get the picture in mind until I started to write it down. Hmmm. So, where does those detailed ideas come from?

082717

Paige likes to eat treats. I went to the kitchen today to eat some figs, and she started to lick my feet because she wanted some of them. So, I went into the room and got her a host of treats of lamb fillings. She ate them up happily! At the same time Forest, our Burmese Mountain Dog/Border Collie mix, came over and sat next to her, very patient, and waited for me to give him some too! Nice! So, I gave him some and he happily ate them.

Now, Paige is greedy and won't share much, so I have to finish feeding her first before she will even share with Forest. Tough. But I am getting it down. She did nothing today besides stand next to where I was giving Forest treats, and she didn't even bark at him! Nice!

Now I am looking at websites online about parallel universes.

111017

Paige has seen a lot of other dogs outside today and has barked repeatedly at them all! She has moved like she is getting ready to sic them and bite them! Interferometer! It is high!

I am going to read some of my *Parallel Worlds* book by Michio Kaku right now. I am at the coffee shop with Paige on the Marine Corps Birthday. Perhaps I will read some about it in that book. We'll see!

Time to read some. Afterwards Krishna, who is also a USMC veteran, is going to take me to a restaurant to get something to eat there.

I forgot to bring the *Parallel Worlds* book with me here, so I am going to look at *The Cosmic Landscape* book instead.

Ok, I have read some of the book, but I am going to leave this part of this story blank of it, because this story is not about a book about quantum theory, it is about Paige, my Superdog! She is very kind now, inside of the coffee shop. The other dog was moved outside the back window and Paige made not one little noise to it. Good Dog!

Now I am wondering what else to write. Paige looks at me constantly in the house, getting a head's up of my condition every time. I look at her a lot too. I try to pet her repeatedly every day, but I feel like it may not be enough. When I do, I get a sense of how many times she wants to be pet and try to pet her enough. My legs hurt when I do it though, so it is interrupted. Too bad! But the concept of me petting Paige until it hurts me is plentiful, and I am sure it earns me respect from Service Dog to Owner.

Paige looks at me with a smile, if you want to call it that, repeatedly every day. I asked her if she understood what I was saying today, and she blinked, which was a "yes!" I love that dog. She is remarkable and friendly and resolute and protective. Yet she almost never barks at people. She has only barked at two of them so far … a guy with a bicycle putting his hand on my shoulder and a Dial a Ride bus driver. The bus driver turned out to be okay, but the bicycler. Paige was ready to bite him! I can't help but to think that he had had some interactions that were highly negative, like assault, on him against another person. And Paige knew it. If that is right, then she can read minds too.

I bet she can!

Paige spends a lot of time reading people's interactions with things. She knows these things with her deepest might, her all-seeing sight, she knows the deepest realms of knowledge about them. She could be a scientist, a physicist, a knowledge-based purveyor or knowledge and know-how. Perhaps I am thinking too much into it. I have gotten signs that Paige is the makings of God. And think about the term "DOG". That is "GOD" in reverse. So, did people come up with the term DOG by realizing that they were elements of God in a narrower form?

That brings one to wondering, what would God be like if he was working in mortal terminology? Would the Bible or the Qur'an still be the same, with the same messages, or would they change over time to a different story? Interesting question, isn't it?

Is it even an element of common sense to wonder how the Bible would change in the first place if God was working differently?

How would that affect how Dogs interact with people?

One question I have is how many more dogs my Service Dog Paige is going to bark at today. I wonder if the number increases sometimes for the purpose of teaching her to hold sway against sicing

111117

That is a lot of ones in today's date, and I am thinking of writing down statements regarding how Paige acts like God. Think about it for a minute.

She is able to sense negative things in other dogs and barks at them. She has sensed people thinking about assault and violence and barked at them. She plays with Forest. She gets down in a get-em position on the ground and waves her tail around. She licks my leg or arm sometimes. She smiles at me. She scratches in the middle of the hallway. Overall, she is a very pleasant dog, with pleasant manners, and I am wondering how many of those things she does in relation to me thinking the way I think about things.

I wonder if she comes up and licks my hand when I am thinking something relevant, like an answer to science questions, for example. Perhaps she plays with Forest when I am coming up with an idea about something. I know she barks at other dogs when she senses that they may want to bite me for no good reason… that one I know of. I could tell by the way the other dogs interact to her barking at them, and the volume and nature of her barks.

So, I am going to write down some of what I am thinking, and what Paige's reaction is to that for further reference.

Right now, I am thinking about what to write next. Paige is laying down, put her head out in front of her and lay it down on the ground. She is in a relaxed position.

"Is that how you want me to be?" I think to her. Her breathing seems like it got a little heavier, but she is laying in the same position. So, we'll have to see what happens when my thoughts become more active. They are lazy right now.

I am trying to think of Gravity right now. I do not know what the particles or elements of it matter the most. I do know that it is based on the weight of the matter that is attracting other matter. Is that a sum of the weight of multiple parallel particles next to each other, close, presenting a certain "pull"? I think it is something like that. That raises the question, "what generates weight?" Is it the function of atoms? I think it is. Different atoms weigh different amounts, so the function of weight must be one of the fundamental probes of measurement. Everything has weight, that I know of.

What if the ability to think is equated on the atomic level, and individual atoms have the ability to think? Then the rules of science would be much different, wouldn't they? Atoms would be able to generate their own weights with thought, and that thought weight would be the one that involved gravity. Interesting, isn't it? Think, that may be the way that people are designed to operate!

Consider if you will, that an atom that wanted to be near another atom would increase its gravity, somehow, so that it would attract the other atom to it. It could be the creation of particles that "drive" the other atom towards it, that are reflected within the format of the atom. It would involve the choice of both the atoms, or multiple atoms of different beings or items.

Scientists may come up with such a thing when they finally find the "Holy Grail" Hadron Tetraquark Particle, which may do it!

112417

It is the day after Turkey Day, Thanksgiving, and we had delicious meals today! My stomach is still full, from yesterday. Yesterday we had pot roast and yams and potatoes and pie for a lunch episode; then turkey, yams, dressing, bread, and something else for dinner. Deeelicious! I am interested in having some more tonight for a snack! I tried to have some today, but all I had for dinner was some turkey and some gravy, and I only ate a little portion of it because my stomach was so full! My plate is in the refrigerator right now, with turkey under gravy in there. Deeelicious, true, but man I was full! Hopefully there will be room in another hour or so.

Paige has been eating snacks from Tony – Krishna's brother. I asked him not to give her any before, but he has a head injury so he doesn't remember everything. He also makes remarks about things that he shouldn't, because he doesn't remember or separate the good from the bad. Too bad!

When she eats people food, she doesn't eat her dog food that is in her dish in my room. Too bad, you silly dog! The reason I don't like her eating people food is because it will give her diarrhea or make her go to the bathroom in the house, and that would be no good. So, I try to keep her from it by not giving her people food. Steaks is one thing I can't resist, true, but everything else I can keep from her. She gets chicken, too, because that is meat and she can eat meat.

It is 7:19PM right now. Paige has been in my room since 6:50PM tonight. She follows my commands really well and comes to the room on her own sometimes without any commands. It is like she knows what the time actually is and where to go and when to go there.

In the last sentence the term "actually is" is underlined. I think it is because the term "is" does not need to be led by the term "actually", so it is perceived as an error. I'm leaving it as it is written, and not correcting it, though.

I have decided upon writing in my "Journal" about science that I am going to put a theory of mine to the test. It involves Paige.

Paige has come across as a Unicorn to me. A Unicorn that has taken on resemblance of a dog's body while still possessing the Unicorn's spirit.

Why would a Unicorn meet with me? Because I was a Unicorn myself, back before I became human. That may be the reason why I know Jesus from the scriptures. He knew Unicorns. Quite simply, I may have been around at the beginning of time, before I shifted memory.

I think I knew Paige before. I recognized her from the time we met.

I am going to be tested on her list of commands. I already know I am going to fail it. I don't go over commands with her very often, and when I do I see that she has already forgotten half of the commands. So, when the teachers see that, they are going to fail me. I hope I don't lose her!

The trainers at the Dog Kennel when Paige was there for our trip to Mexico said she did a really good job on the commands!! So hopefully I will pass the test. It doesn't sound that difficult, and it is supposed to be like it was in the school. That being the case, it must be pretty simple, yes?

The trainers also said she was having no problem with the other dogs at all, too. So, my concerns about her taking up arms against other dogs in the neighborhood may not be what is going to happen during the exercise. I hope not!! The instructors said I could come in there and do some training with Paige and other dogs to get her used to them. I hope so.

They also said that she was hard to groom. They had groomed her while she was there, which is what Krishna and I had talked about before dropping her off, and they said that it was not something we should do again, to get her hair removed. We didn't know. The groomers before had done that on their own. Next time I shall tell them to leave her hair long.

Paige was so happy to see us when we picked her up at the Kennel! She jumped up at first and started to give Krishna hugs and kisses, until the instructors told her to stop. Then she jumped over to me and started to give me hugs and kisses for free! It was so nice! Now I am giving her kisses on the muzzle every single day, and giving her treats to sitting and down, and she likes them. Very nice!

Paige is watching Indiana Jones and the Last Crusade with me right now. She likes it a lot! We are getting ready to go for a walk right now. Krishna has us on hold as she does the dishes in the sink right now. Hopefully, she will be done soon.

Paige likes to walk with me every single day. Twice per day I take her for walks, although sometimes I sleep in in the morning, so I don't take her in the morning sometimes. I am trying to take her more frequently, however. She doesn't seem to mind, however. She is pleasant when she is in the house. She likes me a lot! The exclamation point on that phrase came readily. So, I know, that when it does the computer agrees with what I have written.

She shows no reaction to the commercial where the guy goes up to the girl at the desk and looks at her picture and says: "why isn't she drinking any orange juice?" and she says: "it's because she ran out of her glass of it!"

showing a picture of her standing next to the man with an empty glass in front of her. Perhaps Paige doesn't like that version. Why not? Because it is not that far a locus to think of there being a picture of her getting or doing something that is very negative ... like the girl having nothing to drink in her glass.

Paige, transmit to me something mentally to write about, so that I can put that sort of mental proclivity inside my book about you. The thought of writing is engulfed in colors, namely the color red. What does that mean? Red is the color of blood and injuries, depending on the type of injury. But red on me, could also be the soul! The color is what I am made out of, from the inside out, and it is a color that also amounts to the color of many stars in the sky right now. Spiderman wore red. He is my favorite superhero. Thus, the color red, which is the color of my room I live in, is a heroic color to me, and leads me to believe that Paige wants me to itemize activities written about in such a way as to make them turn into actual actions of the reader!

The thing to start putting here in this file is stories about Paige as a very special Service Dog! She is, too, a remarkable creature. She is a lot like a person. I saw her smiling at me today, to the sound of music. She is playful and fun and interacts in a very friendly manner with Forest every day. I am certain by the sound of the previous paragraph that she knows how to tell me that she can read minds, and she can identify different thoughts within the human realm of thought!

What does the Avengers have to do with Paige's version of the story? Let me see...

She sees the elements of the negative people the way Captain America sees the bad guys within the computer on the ship flying above the earth. That is how. Good. She can use that knowledge to protect me from evil forces. Then Loki comes on and he starts to make people kneel before him. Captain America shows up and begins to combat Loki. The good guys win. That is what will happen when Paige gets involved in a fight among me and some "higher force".

012118

Today was fantastic!

We went to a place called the Montreal Meadows, and there took part in a get-together of graduates of the Service Dog class, it's staff, and the trainers and handlers. It was such a remarkably well positioned time that I don't even know how to describe it all.

Krishna, me, and Paige went. When we arrived, there were other dogs already there, and Paige got along with them all remarkably well! We sat at our table, table #18, which was in the back right side of the chairs and tables there. To our right was outside and out there was a "Smooch your dog" sign on a window in a wall for photos! Down the middle there was a microphone and a movie screen for a show they showed us at the end of the time there.

At the beginning, the lady leading us took the microphone and told us we had three minutes to sit down in our seats. Everyone did on time, which was remarkable. Think of that. People with Dogs were obeying the rules, without hesitation! Then she started to go over the training, and the staff, and then told us about lunch they had made for us and told us to go ahead and get up and go get some to eat from the table.

The food was located on a table in the room on platters. There was potatoes, green beans, salad, tri-tip, and chicken. The meat was deeeeelicious! I wanted to eat a heap of it. I finished a plate and had Krishna get me another one of more meat to eat. I also got some more salad, too! Yum!

Paige sat kindly and nicely while we ate. Then, afterwards, we noticed another dog that looked like Henry. So, I went over to the man with him and asked him if his name was Henry. "Yes, it is!" He said. Krishna and I talked to him a bit and let him know that Paige was his sister.

Then we had our attention brought over to Jane and George, who were Paige's raisers as a young dog. They taught her all kinds of tricks, and they were the source of all her commands. I told them that she goes over the commands really well and is an excellent dog. They were so happy, I cannot explain! Well, I can, actually. Paige started to stand up and give them kissies, because she remembered them and appreciated them! They really appreciated it and were laughing the whole time.

Then I met another lady with a service dog, which was also a Golden Doodle, and I asked her if she was related to Paige. She was! Her name was Claire. So, there was her sister. In addition, the list of actors at the festival had the name of Micah on it, with the Golden Doodle named Chip. At the end of the hearing, we came across a lady who told us about yet another brother, named Kyle, who wasn't there that day, but he was her brother. Interesting!

Then the staff started to give out awards to staff members. They called them up and gave them awards. Deborah and Saliah gave prizes to the staff that worked on the Prison Program.

Then they called up the graduates of the class, and we each, one at a time, walked up there with our dogs and got an award! Even Jonny Cochrane was able to go up there! He was very nice and remarkably kind to us. His dog is named Woody and is a remarkable dog! He told me that he had wanted Paige, but I remember getting her issued to me from the very first day there, so he didn't have access to her. So, the instructors couldn't assess how he did with her. Oh well. He likes Woody. That is an excellent dog and goes well with Johnny.

Overall, the trip was remarkable, and Paige got along fantastically with the other dogs! She smelled and rubbed up against her brother and sister and was extremely happy to see them! I adore that Dog; I do I do! She is a remarkable friend and companion, that is extremely kind and helpful, and shows me the attention that makes me feel ready to be a friend!

012318

Paige is being an excellent girl today. I am at the coffee shop having some coffee, and she is behaving very well, laying down and being quiet. She is interacting very well with other dogs now. She didn't even get interrupted when a commercial with dogs in it came on the TV last night. Nice!

We are going to go outside and wait for Krishna to show up with the car. I am done writing for now.

See ya!

When we went to the kennel to pick up Paige the other day, they gave me a military colored vest for her, with a Canine Support Teams logo on it, and a PAWS, for Wounded Veterans sticker. Very nice! I go everywhere with it on her now. She likes it! She comes into the room to the command "come here" when I give it and gets dressed to go places. A solid dog with a solid vest!

012618

I am trying to find something to write about Paige, and as I wrote this sentence she came into my room and looked at me steadily. Now she is laying on her bed in my room and resting. That is very nice of her to do for me. The one key is not working on my computer right now, though. I wonder if one has to do with the other! Now it is working1! I guess they DID have to do with one another!

How can the presence of my Dog play a role in whether the keys on my computer work right? I do not know. They don't seem related, but they are! Interesting, I say, interesting1!

Paige is looking at me right now. She probably knows that I just wrote about how she took part in the number being able to be printed. She likes me, she does. I like her too. She is a fantastic and interesting dog, with the Canine Support Team's logo on her vest. I wonder, am I going to have to keep on writing stuff about Paige to get the numbers to work?11! I just did, and the numbers worked, so perhaps I will!

This is page 9. The page of Truth. I hope that everything I write here is actual facts!

Perhaps I should pay attention to the page numbers here and write according to the meaning of the number on each page. That would be interesting.

Or perhaps I'll just type.

Paige is laying quietly in my room right now. I think she wants me to keep on writing. I don't know what to write about. She is a very peaceful Dog, and I enjoy her company. I need to write something fantastic for her to peruse. Is that the right word… "peruse"? I think it is. Let me look it up…

"Read something in a thorough or careful way." That is it!

I don't know why some corrections come on the computer for writing, though. Are the words seen as being wrong or in the wrong order? I don't know, I don't know!

I don't sleep. I am wondering if I start to write books on a ready basis, if I will be able to write it when a normal person would sleep, and get it done a lot faster. I don't know. Perhaps I should try it! Will my brain work on that frequency? I don't know! Perhaps I should try it!

I am going to get up and make myself something to eat!

I went into the kitchen and made myself some Karachi, and Paige followed me in and wanted to go outside. So, I let her go while I cooked and ate, and she played with one of her barbecue bones out there. She also dug some in the yard (dammit!), she's not supposed to do that! Then when I was done eating, I went out there in a pair of sandals and socks and cleaned up her poop with the scooper. There was a lot of it!

Then we came back inside the house, and she is laying in the hallway all happy as a clam! She is happy, too, because she made the exclamation point come right out!

It doesn't take much effort to take care of her, that special Dog. There are tasks, like cleaning up her poop, for instance, but it is really simple, and doesn't take a long time. Going places with her is really simple too, because all I have to do is put her vest on, which is really simple, and she helps every time, and it doesn't take a lot of time, either. Then she walks with me wherever I go and is really simple to steer. She doesn't walk rough with me at all!

"Show me my silver lining. Show me my silver lining." That is the song that is on the TV right now.

Paige thinks of the interactions I have with the forces of the universe, I am sure she does. She is a Unicorn, anyways, so it is in her mind. I want to share those abilities with her! "Got a Devil's haircut, in my mind…" That's the song that is on right now. Does that mean that I already have the mental characteristics of Paige? A "Devil's haircut?"

012718

Today Paige has been hacking up hair from the grass she has been eating in the back yard. She coughed up a lot, and I thought she was choking! She wasn't though.

She came to the side room I have there and coughed a bunch of times, then she seemed like she was all right. I hope she is. Troubling how the grass would swell into her throat like that.

I brought her to the coffee shop with me anyways, since she looks like she is fine now.

This is a new line here.

I have been at the coffee shop since 1:20 PM. It is 1:53 PM right now. I am going to be here until 4 PM. I need something to do.

I spend a lot of time watching the workers at the coffee shop. That is because I am unemployed and have been unemployed for the last 13 years. Troubling! I shouldn't have been, you know; but I had to find a semblance of righteousness in the warfare against evil that I took a part in.

It is troubling when people, like doctors, ask me what I did with my time, and I tell them that I was unemployed. The thing is, it happened AFTER I was released from prison, so that plays a big part in it. The remainder is due to the fact that I am disabled from the attempted murder that I survived, so even if I wanted to, I wouldn't be able to work now.

Another element that is disabled is school. Since the incident, I have been unable to drive anywhere, so I cannot drive to school. I tried to go to college with Krishna driving for a while, and took piano classes, but because of my brain injury I began to fail at it! So, I dropped out and haven't gone back to school since then.

I am going to be trying to write a lot more now, now that I am trying to find a circumlocution between time spent writing and time awake. The reason? Because I never sleep now, and I am figuring that my time would be better used if I spent that time writing rather than lying in bed listening to music. For hours at a time. Better to write with that time.

The thing is, I don't know if my brain will be able to manage that kind of data. It may, it may not. Staying awake and writing might actually make me go to sleep, too!

Writing is putting the concept of sleep into my mind, in a way. I am having thoughts about the waitresses of the coffee shop that are heavy on the hallmarks of adaptation. They all seem to be very intelligent, and thus their abilities to adapt to taller orders of existence are hallmarks of their existence.

I should write a story about that.

I just had stories to tell about Paige to Carl at the coffee shop! And foolish me, I don't remember what they were! One was about her getting sick eating grass today, and nearly throwing up. I don't remember what the others were about. I probably have them written down already though.

Here I am going to write down some details about some stories I can write about. Keep in mind, I see no difference between "fiction" and "non-fiction". The laws of science are such that it makes everything possible, over time. And time is the only element of measurement that truly exists.

STORY IDEAS

There shall be a story about a man and woman who start to listen to listen soundly to music, in such a way as to draw mental conclusions about it that gives them a proclivity into the makings of science. They learn how to "see" colors that do not exist and make them move forwards in the universe to the frontal aspects of sight. How do they do that? They ask the question, and the music answers the question with lyrics to special songs! I shall write those lyrics and compose my own songs. Then I shall get them published and made into music.

There shall be a story about a man or woman who can travel through time. They find themselves trapped in a time that is a lot longer than acceptable, so they find a way to transfer their time to a shorter period. How does that work? Look up "time travel" online and look up the theory of it. Apply that theory or those theories. Experiment with it and see if it is actual and can happen in reality! Write down what would happen if it could happen in reality; what the fulcrum of it is regarding the forces of the universe. Think about this in depth and write it in detail!

There shall be a story about a man or woman who can heal as a sense of will. That is the action of a Superhero, isn't it? It is! So, it has probably already been written about in detail, in Superhero or Superheroine books. I shall read about what has been written about that, and put into detail their description, and determine if it seems like it is actual and possible. Somewhere in there is going to be the allowance of the opinion of other Heroes or Heroines, for the purpose of making an accurate and proper decision. What else is involved? What the actual effect would be on the hero or heroine based on science and the effect of what is happening, and the body's effect on it by how it was raised up.

There shall be a story about what happens to the reader when they read a story that has an effect on what actually happens in their lifetime. Make the story a deliberation of effects on the story of their actual life. It should have ramification like that of wind and weather blowing in a disaster, sweeping the effects through the lifetime of the recipient.

That is enough to write about. Details, details, details, my man. Consider what that means.

Then DO IT.

Add in how the job market for low-income people is atrocious right now. There are jobs that are paying people a lot less than what they are worth and can only pay them $3.00 for five minutes of work. Atrocious! That can be a definition of a story – how a company can decide to give the lower income for services for the wrong reason. And they can do it to people who deserve full service, too. It is described as "low paid hell".

012818

I got up out of bed this morning and Paige was in the kitchen trying to sic Sunshiney, who was in her cubicle. The round thing made out of wood and fabric. Sunshiney was hissing and moaning and making a lot of noise. I think she tried to swat Paige from there, when Paige was trying to shove her head into the hole so she could eat Sunshiney! Horrible!

I stopped Paige from sicing her by pushing back on her collar and taking her out of there. Sunshiney didn't get up and leave, however. She was still there! So, I reached in and picked her up and moved her over to Krishna's room to get out of the way. She went readily and barely fought back.

I am worried about Paige. She seemed to WANT to sic Sunshiney! Right now, she is laying in the living room, and coughing and making noise like she is sick. I worry about her, I do!

Gotta get dressed and ready to go to the coffee shop at 1:40PM today.

020318

Paige has acted really well today. There were no dogs out for her to bark at, and the dogs barking at her from other people's yards didn't cause her to bark back. That is a good thing.

We went to the coffee shop, and on the way, she was laying down on the bus, when the driver started to stop really fast, and Paige slid forwards into the cashier device. Then she stood up and didn't want to lay down again. She did though, after I gave her the command to repeatedly. "Down! Down!" So, she got down. Good Dog!

020618

Paige is starting to overreact to me being inside of Krishna's room. There is a gate there, to keep the service dog out, and it interrupts her feelings. She can't come in, but she can see in through the gate. Sometimes she sees the cat Sunshiney, and she gets all hostile when she does. But she can't come in! Only when Forest runs through the gate from the inside and opens it does she come in. Even then she is not supposed to, and so far, I have caught her doing so every time and halted her.

I hope I keep catching her. I don't want her coming into the room and doing something negative to Sunshiney. Like biting her!

I hope Paige doesn't read this and get ideas from reading it!

020718

Paige was really good today so far. This morning, when Krishna and I took her and Forest for a walk in the neighborhood, she saw a big dog barking at us and leaning over a fence. She bolted like she was getting ready to sic him! I help going, and she didn't even bark, even though she looked like she was getting ready to.

We saw another dog on a side street near the end, and she did nothing to him, either. Good Dog1!

I left that 1 in there intentionally because initially I had typed the word "God" instead of "Good", then had to put in the 1's before I was able to put in the exclamation point. I erased the 1's but changed my mind and replaced one of them. So, there it is!

I wonder if Paige is a physical manifestation of God himself, in a female form. That being the case, will she die after 15 years while I am still alive? Hard to say. She is three years old now and will live until she is around 15 years old. I am 43 right now, going on 44, so that means she will be alive until I am 56 years old. That is within the realm of death for me, too, unfortunately. So perhaps she will live longer than I will. Perhaps not. We'll see.

Basically, what happens when a manifestation of God dies here on the planet. Does he move immediately to a different body? Could he occupy more bodies than one at the same time anyways? Probably. Shoot, he has probably occupied people who had moments of good fortune and didn't know why. It was God doing it11!

Right now, I am sitting outside on the bench and writing on my computer on the yard table. Paige is out here and looks very happy. She has gotten very dirty, and Krishna says she smells like ass. I can't smell, so I don't know what she is talking about, but she wants Paige to get washed. Okay, we'll wash her within the next couple of days, I am sure. Krishna is scheduled to work every other day for a week, I think. So, we can go on her off days.

Paige has a sense of what our human time is. I can tell. She has been coming into my room early for rest at night when her time to evolve from the front room comes about. I usually draw her into my room at 7:00PM and close the front door. But she has been coming in here on her own and laying down on her bed around 6:30PM. That is excellent of her to do, and very thoughtful. That Dog has characteristics that read personality all over her!

I went over some of her commands with her today, and she didn't really answer to "Get it" or "hold it". I don't know why. She doesn't have much of a memory for getting items in her jaws and holding onto them. It is a memory to a command that seems like one to remember, but it isn't working out that way. I wonder why.

I am watching TV right now, and it is on commercials instead of Guy's Grocery Games. That gets me to wondering if Paige acts the way she does to me because she is putting into action what she sees in the commercials. She doesn't watch commercials like I do, though, so probably not. Thought I would consider the possibility here. That is what I write about a lot… the possibilities of things going down that are not going down, or that take a creativity of thought to write down.

Do I think or act that way? I don't know, but I know that if I do, and if Paige can read minds like the average Unicorn can, then she knows why I do things so oddly, and she puts that mental process into the reason why she acts towards me the way she does. Which is remarkably. I am going to write about some of those incidents here, and if I can prove that she can read my mind, then I will. And that will prove that I can read her mind too, won't it? It will, it will!

Imagine if I proved in this book that my Service Dog and me could read minds? What would it be worth then? The cooks on Guy's Grocery Games are making extremely hot and spicy food for the judges to eat. That gets me to wonder if my recipe for reading minds will be a spicy one.

I am going to have to write about that subject more and determine what different effects different elements of reading minds has in them. They will not all be the same. Some will depend on what was being thought about by the person whose mind was being read. Others will depend on what exactly was put forth in the mind of the person doing the mind reading. Those options can have a lot of different interlocutions, can't they? Interlocutions has the definition of: a person who takes part in a dialogue or conversation. I think that Paige is a "mental interlocutor".

020918

021318

This damn computer has deleted the last four day's-worth of writings. That troubles me. It makes me wonder if it is going to keep on doing it over and over again. All right, I just saved this to see if it saves.

030118

I screwed up today and ate an extra day's worth of medicines. So, to make up for it, I am not going to eat any medicines tomorrow, if I remember. Troubling...

030618

Paige likes me a lot. She is laying down in the back yard and looking at me resolutely. She is so happy! Krishna keeps saying I should pay her more attention, but she does it when Paige is seeking attention from Krishna! She doesn't realize that Paige moves away from me when I am giving her attention and petting her, which makes me stop. I don't know why. I don't pet her too hard or anything like that, I know that for a fact! So, why does she depart like that?

As I wrote that last paragraph, a bird sitting on the bush next to the fountain started to chase another two birds that are trying to come in and get something to drink. That is like Paige running away from me when I am trying to pet her. In a way.

I wonder if that bird is getting thirsty yet. It hasn't drunk in a long time now. It is still defending the water and refusing to allow any other birds to have any of it.

"I tremble, they're going to eat me alive, if I stumble, they're going to eat me alive. Can you hear my heart beating like a hammer?" Metric

"Maybe I'm all messed up, maybe I'm all messed up, maybe I'm all messed up in you. Woah I wanna wrap it up and lie in it until I m laying down, until I drown. This is the only time I really feel alive. Ohhhh, woahwoahwooahwoah." Nine Inch Nails

"Lahlahdadee dah dah. Lahlahdadee dah dah. Hmmm. Hmmm. When I wake up, in my makup, it's too early for that dress. You better watch out, what you wish for, you better be with this, so much to die for."

The lyrics of these songs will make an excellent addition to the text of my books. I shall look at them as I am writing and add some of them. I wonder, should I make a part of the Graveyard book be a character singing tunes from memory that are solid tunes of real songs? Or should I articulate them differently and write down something different? There are so many fluctuations already understood in the lyrics of songs that it will be extremely hard to change the tunes somewhat in a regular fashion. Oh well. I shall try anyways, I think.

"I'm just a girl, yes I'm some kind of freak, whooah, I've had it up to here. Am I making myself clear?" No Doubt, *Just A Girl*

092318

I have had Paige for a year and a half now. I barely know her age. I keep saying she's 4. She might only be 3 ½. Hard to say. I like her, she is at a good age, regardless!

She is sitting in her usual location in the hallway, and I am on my bed, and she is looking at me steadily. She wants my attention, but I don't know what to do with her to give her positive attention. I like to get up and pet her stomach from time to time, but that only lasts for a little while because I get tired and have to quit. Perhaps I will do it more.

Pops is coming for his birthday. He is three hours away right now, in California city. He had an accident and ran into a deer on the way, and it damaged his car. Hopefully everything is the way he said it was and works properly. He said he was all right. I hope he makes it here okay! I am going to introduce Paige to him when he shows up so that she can recognize him and treat him nicely. He remembers her! Mentioned that she may remember Ladybird, the cat that Pops was caring for here at the house, who died shortly afterwards, and she was cared for by Paige too! That was the best I have seen Paige treat a cat! Very nicely!

Perhaps she will remember that Pops was with Ladybird, too. Paige has a really good memory.

I'm waiting to go to the coffee shop right now. It is 12:17 pm, and I will be getting on the bus to go around 2. The call to Pops was at 11, and he was about 3 hours away, so he may not be here before I go to the coffee shop. We'll see. He has a key, so he can just let himself in. We'll see if he's here within the next hour and 40 minutes. We'll see!

"If I left and they name your friends and you tell your friends and you call your friends baby never mind."

I'm at the coffee shop right now. I am holding back my mind from thoughts of forever and what that means to the equilibrium of existence. Think of the Hereafter for a minute. If everyone who dies goes to the Hereafter, then where are they occupying during their afterlife? Maybe people who die are reborn into a whole new person after death, and they don't know it! How many people on this earth are semblances of others who had existed before them? Is that everyone? Maybe there is no Hereafter… or maybe there is one for people just before Judgement. Yes! Different lives are used to take proper Judgements for the divine recon of Judgement Day! They are weighed as such! And time… time is a vessel for the movement of the actions of those who do the Judgement, and it has a memory that allows it to remove all opposites from it when remembered.

That is applicable to the Service Dog of the *Graveyard* book. She will notice evils on Judgement Day and work to prevent them from taking shape. When she senses someone putting out an evil spirit, she will use her mind to bring to the front the effect of parts of matter flying upwards and floating into the middle of the evil presence, dismantling it and making it non-effective. She can sense bad spirits moving in the atmosphere, and when she does, she will run up and bite them from the air. It will look like she is nibbling at nothing, but she will actually take a part of that bad spirit and crucify it. Now, there will be a part about Jesus's cross in there, about how it was not of the nature used on demons... it was made of a different material... a Good material that allowed Jesus to come back from the Afterlife and live again in another body. Paige has the same DNA as the cross used for Jesus! That gives her the power to do remarkable things to those who are innocent of sins and have been irrelevantly punished in the world! She can bring them to Justice!

It is an adjustment of personality, mostly. When a good person is sinned against in this world, they get funny ideas about what reality is all about... and it effects their decision-making process.

101518

I learned that Paige's dog number is 266650. That number 666 is the number of Satan! And the two before it is the hallmark of the Angels against Satan! So, Paige is a 2 and I am a 2 and we are going to go to Hell when we die to work for Jesus in driving Satan away from us! We shall defeat Satan!

I just read the news that is telling a story about how nearly 50% to 90% of the insects of the Earth have died due to Global Warming. Atrocious! I am concerned that the death on this planet will occur sooner than later, and that creatures like my poor Paige and myself and Krishna and her brothers will be overtaken by those deaths, and possibly even die ourselves! And if it is due to the planet getting too hot, will we be taken to a place that is extremely hot in the Hereafter? Or to a place that is Hell, not the Hereafter? I wonder!

"I'll take, all I ever needed, all I ever wanted. This man, checking me out, sum him on his shoulder. Lady, kneeling in the bedroom, her kneeling is awkwards, too drunk to remember, too drunk to."

101818

We went to Petco yesterday and had them groom Paige and Forest and trim their nails! They look elegant now! They shaved off Paige's face, so she couldn't get as much dirt on it. I asked the cleaner lady if Paige needed me to remove her collar from time to time, and she said that wasn't necessary. So, I bought Paige another collar that is pink with buttons on it and put it around her neck. I put her ID cards on it from her other collar today… one has me and Krishna's phone numbers on it, and the other has the phone numbers to the Canine Support Teams and her Animal Number.

She is so happy with her new collar! And the grooming! We went and spent 30 minutes at the coffee shop today before we went to the Mantra to eat lunch. I had a lamb dish. Paige lay at my feet and slept as we ate. She had gotten snacks of Pupperoni from Krishna before she napped. And she enjoyed it!

Now I'm at home with Paige and she is resting in the living room, napping again with her eyes open. She is such an excellent Dog!

081419

We took Paige to Laguna Beach today. We ate at the Cere de Vie restaurant there and it was delicious. I had some Crepes and Montreal Steak slices, and it came with mushrooms and green pepper slices over the eggs, and they were surrounded by a beautiful sauce! Delicious!

Then when we were done Krishna ordered some Coconut and Lemon Pastries to be made at around 1. Then we went out waiting for them to be made by walking around the beach roads downtown. There were a lot of dogs being walked by their owners, but none of them were by us, at first. We went into a couple art studios and looked at the art there. Then we left a nice one and my leg was hurting and there were benches next to the road and the sidewalk. I told Krishna that I wanted to go back to our restaurant to sit down inside. It was 12:30 and the restaurant was about a 3-minute walk across the street on the other side. She said "No! Sit down here!"

I told her that there were dogs walking around there, and she told me that I was to "Get control of Paige. She is a Service Dog and not supposed to get uptight around other dogs!" So, I got upset, knowing that what she asked of me was not going to happen, but I sat down. Krishna went walking down the corner of the buildings to the other side, looking at shops.

As I was sitting down a man with a dog came walking behind us but didn't pass us but behind me. Paige was moving like she wanted to sic his dog. Then another guy came walking by on the other side of the road with a dog, and Paige began to bark at it. I told her to "Leave it!" Then Krishna called me and said she was at a tea shop and asked me if I wanted some tea there. I said "Yes!" and got up with Paige and started to walk over there. As we went a man came walking the other way down the sidewalk with a barking chihuahua. Paige barked at it and moved like she wanted to sic it. I restrained her. We passed the man and went inside of the tea shop and paid the lady for a tea.

We left the tea shop and I was on my rollator and the tea was hot, so Krishna carried it. We went over by the benches and Krishna wanted me to sit down but I wouldn't do it. I told her that I wanted to go back to the restaurant we had ordered at and wait for her there. She got all upset but followed me there. I sat down and she went to another store, waiting until 1 for them to finish her coconut lemon pastries. She gave me my tea, which was still too hot to drink.

The waitress of the dessert area came by at 12:35 and told me that the pastries were all done and asked how many we wanted. I told her I would ask my roommate, who was in another store. She said "OK!" and that she would wait for her to show up at 1, or before. I told her I would call my roommate.

So, I called her, and she said immediately that she would be over to pick up the pastries. I got off the phone and flagged down my previous waiter, who was excellent, and asked him if I could get a little ice for my tea. He said OK and brought me over a full cup of ice. I used it as Krishna was getting the pastries from the counter and I drank all my tea.

Paige was a good dog. It was only 86% by the ocean, so she wasn't too hot. Now I am at the coffee shop in Temecula, and it is damn 103% outside! And it is in the shade here and still hot. Paige is sleeping with her head laying down. She is exhausted from the heat and walking around. She didn't show it in Laguna, though. There she was a good dog and got some treats from me. When we were eating the waiters brought over some chopped bread and some butter for us to snack on. Krishna gave some bread to Paige to eat, but she didn't want any. So, Krishna put some butter on some bread and gave it to Paige and she ate it up! Then she begged me for some treats as she knows how to do by shaking my hand with her paw, and I gave her some Pupperoni to eat. Three slabs at a time. That is what she has learned that she will get at a time. Often, she will beg me for more treats until I give her three slabs at a time for a total of three or four times. That is what she does when she is hungry and seeking to satisfy her belly. It works, too!

That concludes the trip to Laguna Beach. We were there from 10 to 1. Only three hours. The meal was delicious, and so was the tea, and above all, so was Paige!

We put her in the back of the car and drove back to the freeway home. She lay down in the back and enjoyed the cooler of the car which was on as we drove. Krishna had disregarded the flow of gasoline in the engine and the car was running out. So, to prevent it from running out of fuel she did what Michio Kaku had recommended to the car manufacturer and had turned on the electric emergency power to sustain the car out of fuel for 12 miles. Miraculous! It worked too. We ran out of gas a mile before the gas station, but the car still drove there with no blinking lights or anything. Amazing! And Paige knew it was going to do it because she kept her head down and stayed in a position of rest the whole time that Michio Kaku was put into action.

We made it home okay, and Krishna and I and Paige went inside with Forest. I took off Paige's leash but left her vest on. Krishna changed her clothes for her trip to the hair salon. She didn't take Forest for a walk because it was a whole 103% outside and way too hot to walk. So, when she was dressed me and Paige got into the car with her and we got taken to Ryan Bros. Krishna got out of the car to take Paige really quickly to the shadows outside while I was putting my backpack on and getting my rollator out of the back of the car. When that was done quickly, I went over to the shadows and grabbed Paige's leash. Krishna got in her car and went to her hair appointment, which was supposed to last from 3 to 5.

I walked inside with Paige. It was cooler in there, but still hot. Enough to make me sweat on my arms when drinking some expresso. I sat down and Paige had a water dish set out for her by the staff. She drank out of it for a spell and then I typed some on this file about Paige on my computer. As I typed, she came over and tried to shake my hand. So, I shook her hand back and gave her three treats. She gobbled them down, then stared at me for a spell with her paws on the ground. Then she raised her left paw back up and shook my hand again. She wanted more treats! I gave her three more nibbles and she was happy, somewhat, but still hungry. She begged again, and I gave her treats again. That time it was enough. She lay down and put her head down and acted like she was going to sleep. It was 3:30 pm… about half an hour before her dinner time. That is why she was so hungry. She needed to fill her belly somewhat. And that is what I did, because I am used to her habits!

Michael and Jerry, the new owners of the coffee shop, came by today and started to paint the building. Michael came over and talked to me. I told him that I was writing a story about Paige, and he said it would be really good if I could get published. I agree. I told him it was only on page 18 though and told him about how I had not written anything in it since around month 9 of 2018. Today it is the 14th of August 2019. He thought that was funny, and that I could come up with things to write about her. I immediately got to thinking that I was going to write about the things that I do in Paige's company, which is mostly writing or reading, and I was going to write about the subject matter of science that I was writing about. I'll go more into that later, because it is true that Paige is a Genius with extraordinary powers that one would think a dog doesn't have… but she does! And it is starting to show!

Then I spoke to Michael about science. I told him that I write about it a lot in my journal. He asked what it was about, and I said: "It's about how Parallel Universes work." We discussed Parallel Universes a bit and he mentioned how it had something to do with measurement and time travel and such things. His responses were really intelligent, and it was clear that he had spent a lot of time thinking about such things.

I also mentioned that I wrote about Quantum Theory and how it is to become unified with Relativity, by Einstein. I mentioned the main authors that I read… Michio Kaku and Brian Greene and how they are both into physics and had helped to develop String Theory. I told him that String Theory had evolved to the higher mathematics of M-Theory and so far, that is the only theory that is unifying the mathematics between Quantum Theory and Relativity. Thus, it may be an accurate answer to the unification of the two.

"That would be interesting to look into", I told him. He agreed.

Then Michael dismissed himself because he and another guy were going into the men's bathroom to paint it a brighter color and to fix the lights. That is very good of them, and I told him so. I really like Michael and Jerry. They are both fantastic people and are already doing a lot to improve the atmosphere of the coffee shops existence.

Paige and I waited until around 4:45 PM for Krishna to come back. She got out of the car when she arrived and came over to the shadow to get Paige and to bring her in the heat to the car quickly, and Paige went along readily and quickly. I don't think her feet burned. She showed no sign that her feet were burning.

At home with Krishna and Paige, I was in Krishna room with them and Krishna was watching a stupid jewelry show that she watches all the time, and I asked her if she had ever thought of Quantum Physics. She responded rudely: "No! I am watching this (stupid) show!" Then she replied: "Ask Paige if she understands!"

So, I did just that.

"Paige, do you understand Quantum Physics?" I asked her, and she immediately put up her paw to shake my hand. Then after a minute up she put it down. So, I asked her: "Paige, do you know about Relativity?" And again, she raised her paw for a handshake!

The proof is in the pudding... Paige is a Genius that understands the higher effects and theories of science!

Now it is time to go to sleep. Paige is laying out in the hallway, head down, like she is asleep. I am going to put my computer away and try to think of what else I am going to write about Paige. I want to start to read over my Relativity book by Einstein and talk about the details of the theory with Paige and see what her reactions are. Perhaps they will be something worth writing about. I think that they will be!

Good night.

I am at the coffee shop that I go to now. It is morning on 081519. Paige is behaving really well. She is following me readily and happy. I am writing on my laptop right now. I shall write down what I am going to write about.

I am studying the 4 laws of physics that pertain to everything we know about. I am also going to break out my book on Relativity to get a symbiosis of what it is all about. In the process I am probably also going to look up Quantum Theory and see if I can draw any conclusions about that and Relativity. That would be a tall order because it hasn't been done yet. And in the process, I think I am going to start to relearn mathematics so that I can apply at least some Calculus to it. Those are tall orders of thought… some of the highest there are. I have nothing but time to peruse them, though. I am unemployed due to my disability and have been since 2006. I have plenty of time to peruse those things.

I was given a dish of water for Paige right after I

arrived at the coffee shop. The waitress who gave it to her holds my highest respect and does a fine job on serving me. She says all kinds of nice things about Paige too! That is so nice of her. She is fantastic.

Paige is laying under the table with her head down now. She does that and looks like she is sleeping but when you look at her face you see her eyes are open. So, she isn't asleep... just pretending. Interesting! "I was just sitting in the back seat smoking a cigarette that you thought would be your last, and guess what? I was falling deeply, deeply in love with you. And we never would have known until just now!" That song was just on the radio at the coffee shop. It plays into how I feel about Paige!

I am home now. We went to lunch with my friend from the coffee shop named David. He is a preacher that said a lot about religion to my roommate. He is a Christian and asked her what religion she was. She told him she was a Muslim. He talked about Jesus a lot and accepted her religion. That was nice of him! I haven't told him yet... but I am a Christian, Buddhist, Jewish, Muslim, and Hindu. I believe in all of them because I believe in Parallel Universes and believe that such differences in the laws of physics allows for different things to happen to different people for different reasons. That is what I believe...

I am reading about Relativity on Wikipedia right now. I will write about it after I finish. I shall also ask Paige what she thinks about the theories when it comes time to ask her. Remember her putting up her paw when I asked her if she understood Relativity. That tells me that she is a Genius with answers! We'll see what they are.

I read about Special Relativity on the Relativity Wikipedia site. I don't remember much of it, so I am going to have to read over it again before I talk to Paige about it... because she probably knows everything that I would ask of it!

So, until then... another break...

081619

In 9 days, on the 25th, we are going to see Gary Sinise in Newport Beach Jewish Temple. He is giving away his recent book to the veterans that go. Nice! Me and Krishna get to go for free too because we are both veterans! That is also nice! Sinise played Lieutenant Dan Taylor in Forrest Gump. That was a fine movie. There will be other veterans with Service Dogs there probably, too. That will be interesting. As long as they are Service Dogs Paige will not bark at them or try to sic or bite them. I prefer that.

Today Paige was a really good dog. She came into my room while I was waiting for Dial a Ride to come and pick me up for a trip to the coffee shop. She let me put her vest on readily about an hour before the bus was supposed to arrive. Then she raised her paw and tried to shake my hand. I shook it and got a treat out for her to eat, but she wouldn't eat it. She stared at the TV instead. She even knocked a piece out of the three I had in my hand and knocked it onto the floor.

I left the one on the floor there for her to eat, eventually, if she wanted to, and put the others back in the pouch. Then she raised up her paw and shook my hand again. I pulled out three more treats and once again she didn't eat them. So, I thought about it and wondered: "What is the reason for her to come and shake my hand if she doesn't want treats? Is she thinking about the science things I asked her yesterday?"

So, I asked her: "Paige, are you shaking my hand because you want to talk about Relativity?" And as I did she wagged her head from side to side, like time travelling at light speed and being sensed, and then put her head down and ate the treat that was on the ground…which was telling me that the Relativity question was indeed why she was shaking my hand and taking no treats.

Interesting.

I think that most people wouldn't believe it, because they don't have the same intelligence that I have. So, they see things differently and wouldn't put together the details of that episode. But I did, and to me it shows that Paige is extremely intelligent and wants to communicate with me about intelligent things! Just feeding her is good, true, but not enough. It definitely doesn't equal thinking about such things like the speed of light being the fastest force there is and everything else being faster is impossible…

or so the scientists think. Nothing has been tested to be faster than the speed of light. Nothing. Paige knows this and wants me to talk about it so she can respond the way that dogs do.

We went to the coffee shop and she lay down there and did very little. It was hot, but not in the 100% range. It was in the 90's. That is still hot for her.

We're home now and she is in her resting position on the floor. So is Forest. He is in my room on Paige's bed laying like he is asleep. He is 18 years old. That is up there!

That's all I have to write today. I am getting ready to eat some hamburgers that are now ready.

081719

I am at the coffee shop right now with Paige. I take her everywhere I go, except the movie theatre. It is too loud in a movie theatre for her to lay down and be calm. And they do previews with dogs in them and that makes her bark. So, that is a no-go and I don't take her to the movies.

Paige misses me when I am at the movies without her. She is a very protective Dog and misses her client when he is not around. So, I try to do my best to stay around her. I don't go to the movies very often unless it is a movie that I really want to watch. There hasn't been one like that for months now, so that is good. The last movie I went to go see was about a Dog that got lost from his house and went running for about a year in the wilderness before he found his way back home. He almost got hit by a car crossing the street back to his house! But he made it. His father was a doctor or a nurse or something at the hospital of town. That is where he was reunited with them. Paige wouldn't have liked the movie because it had a Dog in it that did a lot of things. So, she would have barked. So, I left her at home.

When I got brought home, my roommate had left Paige at the house, so she wasn't in the car. When I got home Paige was bouncing and all excited to see me. My roommate told me that she had given Paige a treat of a meatstick to calm her down while waiting for my return... so she wouldn't act up. She was satisfied, and really attentive to me when I returned. She put her ears on my hands and flexed them around and rubbed her head on my leg and shook my hand with her paw repeatedly. She was so happy to see me, she was smiling!

What a darn good Dog!

I pet her on the neck and said good things to her about the movie, telling her about the plot and what it had to do with her, being about a Dog and all. She really liked it. And that was what I had come to expect from her... a nice understanding of my experiences. She is a really intelligent Dog!

Now I shall create a new chapter, now that I have

covered what a period of two years and five months was like with Paige in my company. The new chapter shall be about what it was like to get Paige, from my memory of it, and what the 2-week course was like that I attended to become her owner. It was intense, accurate, ready, and necessary. And I graduated it nicely! Very good!

Read on, and you can use that information if you yourself choose to go through Canine Support Teams to get a Service Dog in your name and thus attend the class on them, like I did. It will be very useful, I hope!

MARCH 2017 CLASS FOR ME TO GET MY SERVICE DOG PAIGE

I got Paige from the Canine Support Teams Incorporated inside of Murrieta, California. Paige was born there at a house, and I don't know if because of privacy rights if I can put her raiser's names in here, so I won't. I have met them. They are really nice people and great puppy raisers.

Canine Support Teams has a classroom on a ranch made for the possession of Service Dogs on it. There is a dirt road going into a gated fence around the parking lot, which is small. Next to the parking lot there is a building that is a kennel with cages in it for the Dogs to sleep and rest in. On one side of the kennel there was a field with a fence all the way around it that was made for the Dogs to run and play in. On the other side there was a sidewalk leading to the classroom inside of a different building. I shall tell you about the classroom.

In the front door of the building there were a couple of sitting chairs next to the door on the inside, and next to them was a table with about 12 chairs around it for the students, and some open space between the table and the kitchen for the Dogs to sit and play and snack and get things. There was a TV on a stand in the learning room that had a video player attached to it for instruction.

That was the room that I was introduced to the first day in March 2017 that I was there. There were about 11 other students, filling up all the chairs that were there. There were no Dogs in the building, yet. The instructors came over and began to teach.

We students were introduced into what the classroom was all about and what we were to learn there. We were told that we were going to be interviewed about things like our job and our living arrangements for a Service Dog. We were told that a Service Dog was trained to go with us everywhere we went to, except the Hospital, where Service Dogs were only partially allowed and not during surgery… but we were to take them with us everywhere. When we had a Service Dog picked to be ours and we passed the test we were to receive a card with the laws regarding Service Dogs stamped on it, with a picture of us with the Service Dog on the cover. That would be so nice, I thought!

I shall write some more about what the stamp on the

card says about taking a Service Dog everywhere except the Hospital with me, at the end of this chapter.

After briefing us on what the training was all about there for the next two weeks the instructors called us up to them one at a time to ask us questions about our living arrangement.

The instructor I had called me over and had me sit down in a chair next to her. She said she was going to ask me questions about living arrangements and Dog commands. I remember that she asked me what our house was like and if we had a back yard for the Dog. "How big is it?" she asked. I told her that it was small, but big enough for the Dogs to run around and play and poop and pee. She said that was good.

She knew that I was a former United States Marine and that I had special training. So, she asked me about what commands I used in the military. I told her that I used to be in Force Reconnaissance Company, which is the most elite force in the Marines. "It is like Special Forces", I told her. "The commands were really elegant. We had to do things like Call for Fire from Artillery on enemy forces from a distance on the radio. That was detailed and necessary. Distinct commands." She appreciated that.

"What are you doing for employment?" She asked me that next.

I had a mental injury from Solitary Confinement in prison, when I was there from 2007 to 2009. Then I had severe brain injury from the incident in 2013 that caused me to petition for a grant to get a Service Dog from Canine Support Teams in 2015. I was disabled from that as well, and unable to work since 2006, in prison. So I told her that I was unemployed because I am disabled. "I write books on my computer," I told her.

She left it at that. She then told me that "we pick the Dogs that the students train with on a day-to-day basis. The Dog can change depending on how you interact with them. We want the Dogs to have the same personality as the owner. Based on the fact that you are an author, who write pages of books, we are going to give you a Dog that fits that profile. You are going to start out with a Golden Doodle named Paige. A Golden Doodle is a Golden Retriever as one parent mixed with a Poodle as the other parent. Both of Paige's parents were big Dogs, so she is big as well. Enjoy, and I hope you do well with her!"

That concluded the interview. She told me that the next thing that was going to happen was that we were going to go over Commands for the Dogs, as a class. We were not going to get a Dog that day... training with them was going to start the next day. And we were only going to train with them for the first week for half a day at a time, then they were going to be allowed into the yard to play while we did more classes on the TV. I said that was "OK"! And I went back to the table.

My roommate was coming to class with me. She had taken time off of work to attend, since we lived together, and she was also going to be around the Dog a lot. So, she sat next to me.

We waited for the rest of the 11 students to sit in their interviews, then an instructor came over and turned on the TV. On it was a picture with words on it that described the commands that we were to give our Service Dogs. We had been told that we would be giving them commands for our test and would be graded on how present and accurate they were. So, I wanted to learn my commands for the Service Dog because I am an Active Learner and had learned to perform well in Force Reconnaissance Company! Keep in mind that I was working on a Special Forces mindset, but that doesn't mean that YOU have to reach that same level of mindset to be a Service Dog owner! It just helped my case out… but it is not required by any means!

The screen with the Commands on it had the commands listed in the order of importance… which seemed at a random order because they were ALL important. Next to the listed command there was a description of what the command meant, about one or two sentences worth of information. It describes at the very beginning what the commands were meant for. They were to drive the Dog into doing items or tricks that an obedient Dog would do when receiving the verbal commands from the owner. Thus, the command would happen, and the Dog would want to do the trick readily and do them. And I was sure it would work out that way too, for the work that had to be put into making the screen on it on the TV in the first place.

Then when that class was over, we had another class. This one was on the special characteristics some of the Dogs had. I learned there that Paige had the ability to provide recompense for Post Traumatic Stress Disorder (PTSD), which I have from the military. I also have it from being a victim in 2013 of attempted homicide against me. I had been in a coma for 2 months and unconscious for about 8 months total. Then I recovered and put in for my grant for a Service Dog. It was nice to know during that class that Paige and many other Dogs has been trained to provide protection for their owners. They would bark at or bite whoever was trying to assault or do something negative to the owner or them. That was a great reaction, I thought. It was precisely what I had needed when I was the victim of homicide! Paige was trained to help me out with all those things.

The instructors told us that many of the Dogs came from the organization of PAWS for Wounded Veterans. They were trained in the specialties of military forces and veterans and thus were trained in how to handle PTSD and mental trauma and other illnesses of military service. Thus, they were trained in how to help us.

Many of the Dogs had also been a part of the Prison Pups Program, where they spent some time being trained under the auspices of a prison inmate and their trainer and learned how to perform under stress. The prison inmates did a really good job with them! Amazingly well. Thus, all the Dogs at the training kennel for the course we students had to take on the Service Dogs were really good and well trained in how they handled their students... which were to become their owners, if the circumstances were right.

Those elements were all included in our class about the Services our Service Dogs could offer. Then we got a class about Hazards, which included the Dog biting or barking at a person. We were supposed to use the leash to keep them from biting a client or person. They could bark though, although we would say the words "Leave it!" to them to get them to try to stop. It worked most of the time. Most. Not all. Paige never wound up biting anyone. She let the leash control her.

Then the classes were over, and we were prepared, as students, to take our Dogs the next day. So, we departed and got in our cars and went home. The instructors were really good and asked us before we left if we had any questions and stuck around answering questions from the students as needed before the students went home, or out, or wherever. Many of the students were former military and had been in the Marine Corps or the Navy... which are the two main forces down here by San Diego. The Marines serve on Camp Pendleton, California and the NAVY on bases by San Diego and Coronado Island. They asked a lot of questions and were very kind with the answers!

That concludes the first day. Now, onto me meeting Paige!

The next day I went back to the kennel of Canine Support Teams Inc. and was met by the kennel by the staff. They went over to a cage and opened it up and got out an excellent-looking Golden Doodle. She had no vest or collar on her, but the staff put a collar on her and connected a leash to it. Then they brought her out.

"This is Paige," she the instructor said. "Enjoy her!" So, to that I thanked her and walked Paige into the classroom. There were other students around getting their Dogs as well.

I sat down at the end of the table because that was the only seat open at the time. So, that was my seat, at the head of the table! Paige sat down next to me. I was walking with a cane because my legs had been broken and I needed it for stability. Paige knew about the misbalance I had and adjusted how she walked with me accordingly, so that I wouldn't fall. The Dog seemed remarkable from the moment I had her. My roommate sat down next to me and Paige and the TV and asked me questions about what I had been taught. I told her that she was there, so she knew already what I know about it. She laughed and stopped asking. Then she started to ask me questions about Paige, like: "How often do you give her treats? Can she turn on a light bulb? What does she do for tricks?" I couldn't answer her because I had never had Paige before and that was the first time I had her in my presence!

Then the instructors started the class. The classes were 2 ½ years ago and I had brain damage at the time of the classes, so I don't remember exactly what they were all about. But I remember the pattern. The instructors would give us the Service Dog that they were trying us out with the first thing in the morning. Then we would go to the classroom and they would give us a class. Then we would take the Dog outside and walk with them or tell them to "go now" so they would go to the bathroom outside or we would experiment with treats with them, after the class on it was done. We arrived for this for 5 days then took a 2-day break on the weekend before our final days at the Mall. During each day the instructors would teach us calibration to handle the Service Dogs called DOGMAS. They were listed in the 100-page instruction manual that they gave us on the course we were taking.

I recommend it if one is getting a Service Dog! It was created by Carol Roquemore, the creator of Canine Support Teams and it is in-depth on the course. There was another instructor named Debrah, whose last name I have forgotten, and one named Shari Butterworth. They were both remarkable instructors. Carol was disabled and rode in a wheelchair, but a remarkable owner of a Service Dog herself! Look her up online if you are interested. Check the "Founder" link on the Canine Support Teams Inc. website.

From there, the first day we started to get classes on the Service Dog. We started out with a list of some of the Commands for the Dog. Then we went over the DOGMAs, which is a protracted measure of capability and character of the Dog that is highly accurate and essential. The DOGMAs covered survival instincts of the Dog, how to handle them, how to treat them, and what their character is like, among other things. Then the class went into lessons, the first 5 days teaching about three lessons per day. The lessons covered everything one would need to know about handling and raising a Service Dog.

The instructors made it clear in the lessons that Service Dogs are Caregivers… not Pets!

We also learned during the Commands session how to treat the Dog. We learned things like the command for having them go to the bathroom if they had to go outside, to lay down and go to sleep, to turn on the light or turn it off, to get a goodie and hold it in their jaws, to eat a treat, and so on and so forth.

I am not going to go over what the DOGMAs were in the book. There was 100 pages in that book, and I am not going to replicate it. I am reading over it right now to see what I have forgotten. The student of Canine Support Teams gets a copy of the book during their admission phase of the class on the first day, so they can make copies of it for later perusal. All one has to do is sign up for a class, or to go to the Canine Support Teams Inc. website and go to "Contact" and send them an email asking for a copy. I am sure they will provide one! They may charge you admission prices to the class if you are not a veteran of the military, though, but it isn't much. You would get it for free if you were a Veteran. I am a

Veteran of the United States Marine Corps, so they gave me the class for free. And in regards to my Service Dog Paige, I was a victim of homicide by the VA Hospital in Phoenix, Arizona, which I am suing for it, and because of that victimhood the Canine Support Teams provided me a Grant for free and raised Paige for 2 years without charging me anything. And it cost them over $8,000.00 to raise her! And that was for free for me! So nice of them! You would be able to get the same Grants if you were disabled from the military, which a lot of people are.

I also have PTSD from the military. When I was in Force Reconnaissance, we were coming home from deployment in Hawaii and got word there that 7 Force Reconnaissance Marines had died from another platoon doing the same exact training that we had done on board the USNS Pecos. Their helicopter had caught a leg in the barrier around the flight deck and went spinning upside down into the ocean, causing 7 of those Force Reconnaissance Marines to drown. We still had a deployment to do and were planning on going back to that ship to do more helicopter inserts and extracts on it. We also had a lot of helicopter rides to take in training before the Pecos. The training was tough, because me and a lot of other Marines that were in the platoon were thinking about ways that we could die and have nothing we could do to stop it as we trained... and it developed into a mindset of "imagining" that we were dying in the helicopters and taking action to prevent things like drowning... which really wouldn't work. I developed PTSD from it.

I had episodes of PTSD after the incident in 2013, where I would get ideas in my head that were extremely negative and disruptive, and my arms and shoulders would shake. But Paige had been trained in PAWS for Disabled Veterans and the Prison Pups Program, and in those two she learned how to handle a Veteran with PTSD. She would see me having an episode and come over to me and immediately start to lick my arm or my leg, wherever the episode was apparent, and it would immediately calm me down and show me support. That is such a good Dog! To be honest with you, at first, I thought there was nothing that could be done to stop an episode... but then Paige came along and showed me otherwise. That is such a great thing for her to do for me!

Now I shall go on to explain, in general, what the training with Paige was like. The semblance of the first 5 days in the classroom will be separated from the part about the training around and inside the Mall, and the final test and graduation.

I shall go over the training and the classes that I had here, without going so far in-depth with it that it goes into what was written in the Canine Support Teams Instruction for Assistance Dogs Program Training Manual. It shall go into generalities of what the training was like with a few examples... enough to get the point across... and examples of what my mindset was like during the training. That will help the reader draw a conclusion as to what their mindset will be like during a similar course for them, and hopefully will help them prepare their minds for such an exercise. I am not going to separate many days. The exercises were all basically the same for the first 5 days of the course, which was held in the classroom and the walking area around the kennel of the Canine Support Teams compound. Then we had a couple days off to go home without the Dogs. Then we went and spent the next 5 days leading up to the final test at the Mall doing nothing but exercises with the Service Dogs and going over, by word of mouth, the DOGMAs that were involved that day. I will only generally and roughly go over them with you here. If you want a full description of them, you can get a Manual and read it.

Now, a general description of what the first 5 days were like in the classroom, and around it.

We started out by going into the kennel to get our Dogs then headed over up the walkway on the outside to the classroom. I sat down next to Krishna at the head of the table with Paige and was right next to the TV set. The instructors were all there in the kitchen and said hi to us students. The other students came into the classroom and sat at their seats. Some were female, others were male, and most of them were veterans from the military and all of them were disabled in some way, including me.

When we were all in there the instructors turned on a video of words on a screen that was the DOGMAs of the Dogs. Those are universal concepts behind raising a Service Dog that are all precise and excellent in their availability. In the book it covered the DOGMAs one page per day for the first 5 days. They mentioned things like "RESISTANCE" in the Dog and how to handle it (in many different ways and terms), giving them treats, and the exchange of personality characteristics. I am not going to mention the individual DOGMAs here… you can read over them yourself as a student for a Service Dog, or, perhaps, I haven't read them yet but I saw that there were over 40 different books written about Service Dogs, and you could get one of those books by looking them up online under the search "books about Service Dogs" and read over the details of it.

The screens of the TV had a DOGMA term listed, and next to it was a dash then the definition of the term. Each screen covered a whole page of the Canine Support Teams Manual.

That covered, the next screen came up and we had a break. The next screen had the Commands listed in order with the definition of each next to the Command. We could read over them on the break, and me and Krishna talked about them to determine which was the most accurate of the ones listed. They all seemed accurate, but I was going to have to try them out to see what the Dog's response to the Command was. I figured it was pretty obvious, because the Commands used regular words that made sense in a particular action. But I wanted to make sure I knew what the animal was going to do.

The instructor then started to address what each of the Commands were and what they would do for the Dog. The description of the details of the Commands described what they would do accurately. We were told that we could copy a handful of pages of flyers and it would cover all the Commands for us to have for our own perusal. So, after the first day there, that is exactly what I did. I printed out about 5 pages of Command-Description list. I still have it some 2 ½ years later.

Then the class was over each day and the instructors told us that it was time for us to use the detail of the Commands list and give our Dogs certain commands. The Commands we gave to them varied each day. For example, on the first day we were to give them their name, "PAIGE" to be followed by the Command "SIT", during which the Dog would sit down calmly, or "DOWN", during which the Dog would lay on it's belly and keep it's head and paws down. There was also the command "MOVE", which would lead the Dog to follow you somewhere. Another day there was a command of "LIGHT", which drew the Dog to turn a light on or off. There was also "DOOR", which was to lead a Dog through an open door. On yet another day we had the Dogs in the classroom and put out a cord or an iPhone and told them to "GET IT", and they took it in their jaws. "HOLD" followed that command and to that they would hold the object in their jaws. Then "GIVE IT" would follow, and the Dog would put the object down in your hand or on the ground and leave it there. Then we went outside to a table out there with a bench around it and told the Dog "INSIDE" to get them to go under the bench and lay down. That was what we were supposed to do with them in public places. Then we told them "OUT" and they got out into the open. Then we told them "UP" and they jumped up onto the tabletop and rested there. To that they responded to the Command "DOWN" as well to get down from the tabletop. They are such intelligent Dogs you would not believe it until you see it. They responded very well to all our commands and liked to train with us!

It took about two hours for all of us students to give the Dogs our Commands. We could only do it one at a time with the instructors watching us and correcting us, so that took some time. The rest of the morning was spent doing DOGMAs and getting briefed on the classes we were having that day. Then the afternoon came. We took the Dogs out during lunch to go to the bathroom, as most of them had been trained to do at that time, and then we took them back over to the kennel and put them in it to rest in their cages. While waiting for the kennel to open many of us took our dogs to the fenced yard to walk around and play with the other Dogs. They really enjoyed that. And they went over to the kennel readily.

We students left for lunch. There were drive-through restaurants open down the street from the school. We went there and got some food-to-go and brought it back with us to the classroom to eat at the table. There was time for us to drive out there to get the food and to bring it back with us and for me and Krishna to eat it at the classroom before class started again. Granted, we weren't usually done before class started again because we had lessons that were scheduled for 2 to 3 lessons per day for the 5 day period, but we could eat while we were watching them on the TV and listening to the speeches given by the instructor staff.

The lessons covered a lot of stuff. They were all about raising to Dogs and went into detail about the remedies for problems and how to handle resistance in the Dogs.

The first lesson covered the orientation to the Canine Support Teams Training Camp. It covered a general summary of what was going to be covered, what was going to be taught, what exercises there were to handle the Dogs, it covered that we were going to learn the Commands of the Dogs and to put them into action. Then it went to lesson 2, which covered the Orientation to the Canine. It covered how there is a semblance of Odor, Motion and Movement that dictate a Dog's personality… his or her Orientation. Then the third lesson starts, and it is titled Survival Needs for the Dog and yourself. It is necessary for the Dog to satisfy its instinct for self-preservation and for you as it's owner to stay healthy. There are a few features listed that go into it, but it isn't as large a lesson as the part about Orientation of the Canines or the Orientation of the Canine Support Teams Training

Camp. Those parts of the lesson were really long… longer than any others in the book!

The next lesson, for day 2, starts out with a part called Canine Motivators. That part goes into the mindset of the Canine and ways that an owner can get the good graces of the canine in their order. Things like A Game or Play or a Food Treat gets a canine's attention and a good standing on their part. My Service Dog really likes the treats, and when she gets hungry, she begs for them by shaking my hand and looking in my eyes. She is such a good Dog. A GREAT DOG! The next lesson discussed the Rules of Praise, which is what a person is supposed to give their Service Dog if they follow a Command rightly and do it accurately. A person gives them some praise, verbally and possibly with a pat or pettings and the Service Dog smiles at them! That was a good part of the lesson. Then the next part was about Resistance. That is what a Dog does when it doesn't want to do something, or it is in a bad mood. There was a lot in that part about how to handle resistance. Then the lesson goes into the Grooming part of the lesson. That talks about how a Dog is to be Groomed and what occurs at the Grooming Pet Place where they are getting done at. It discusses what an owner is to do if they are grooming their Dog themselves and the steps that they are to take to get it done properly.

Man, it is taking time for me to read over these lessons to write about them.

The next section of the Lessons covers the Vet Lecture. By "Vet" they mean "Veterinarian". The list in the lesson is numbered by topic and there are 42 different topics listed. They cover how to analyze your dog for damages, how the vet analyzes the dog, what to do in the event of frostbite or snakebite or other things that can happen, and many other things. I am not going to list them here. You can get a book and read it yourself. The next section in the Lesson is about The Wheel. The wheel is a picture of different personality and expectations of the master and the dog, with one type on one side (like "aggressive") and the opposite on the other side (like "submissive"). The master is expected to help to draw the dog to move towards an equal version between the two separations. The dog is supposed to be in the middle, and it is up to the handler to bring them to those conclusions.

The Day 4 Lesson starts out with pages written about Emotionality of the handler and the Dog. Then it goes into a part titled Home and Public Safety. I shall cover them briefly herein.

Humans think, a lot, but dogs don't think a lot... they react. They react to threats and treats and food and play and aggressiveness and whatever stimulation there is for them. They can react positively to positive things or negatively to negative things. Dogs are predominantly emotional animals. They have a sense of dependence because they can't do things like feed themselves without help with someone getting the food for them. Some would argue that and say that Dogs could hunt like the

Wolves do, but that throws away development of DNA in the dogs that lead to it... which many would say is not present in may types of dogs. Dogs also have a sense of Rejection when they aren't accepted or don't get treats and petting and such. Dogs that are abused show the mental proclivities of an abused child because they have been rejected too much and start to soil the ground everywhere and pee and bite and bark and do things that are negative to the abusive handler. The CSTADPTM explains all this in detail on its 5 pages of information on the subject. Then it goes into Home and Public Safety.

Home and Public Safety covers when the Dog has to go to the bathroom, what is it's handler to do for those circumstances, how a person is supposed to carry a poop bag on them to clean it up when time calls for it, what the procedures are for leaving one's dog alone are, and what to do if a place violates the law and denies a disabled handler access with their Service Dog to a place or facilities. There is a calling out against that, and steps for the handler to remedy the situation without being obstructive.

That concludes day 4. Now I shall finish the Lessons section with a diatribe about Day 5. It starts with a part called Correction, which is the handler telling the dog when something is inappropriate for it to do. To correct an action a handler needs to be forceful with the dog and tell them "No!" to get them to stop. It can be followed by another command which is separate from the negative action taken.

When correcting a dog the handler is never supposed to show anger or frustration, because that will be read by the dog and the dog will continue or enhance the negative action in response to the anger. That is no good. Instead, the handler should use the Command "No" or "Don't" and keep their voice firm but calm. When a correction is called for the handler should have an upbeat, positive, smiling tone to share their determination for positive action with the dog. They will listen!

Then the Lesson covers the dogs Learning Theory. This Lesson goes into detail on how a Dog is trained to do certain things. For example, it goes into the Command of "Sit" and what is done to get an inexperienced Dog to do it. It goes into detail on how to do it and give the commands and to make the dog go it with action in order to give it the experience… and when and how long to wait between Commands to give it a chance to follow the Command. The Lesson also goes into the psychology of the dog during the training, which is important to the handler to know. And Dogs sometimes model the behavior of other dogs that they see, doing things like getting water or peeing in a bush. The Dogs see that behavior and sometimes mimic it.

The Lesson goes into how the Dogs equate the learning process together into a solid Theory of Behavior that they follow over time. They learn about Commands and what they mean through thought to the sounds, thought to the behavior wanted, and action on their part. It is extremely detailed.

That concludes my introduction to the Canine Support Teams Assistance Dog Program Training Manual. If you are interested in getting a Service Dog for yourself, if you are handicapped or injured or have certain mental disorders, or definitely a Veteran of the Armed Forces, then you are available for becoming a member of the class of students to get a Service Dog for your own. It only requires some patience on your part, some studying, and the ability to take your Service Dog everywhere you go (except the hospital)… and that is definitely acceptable if you like Dogs! Try it, and you will like it!

Now I shall tell you about what the Commands were like to give to Paige, and my emotionality at giving them and leading her for the first few times.

I am writing this some 2 ½ years after the event happened, so I may have it out of order. But I remember the events, somewhat. I shall write down what I have in memory here. I am going off of the list of Commands inside the *Canine Support Teams Assistance Dog Program Training Manual* (CSTADPTM), and that was what we used in the class at the beginning of each day, so it is a reminder of what Commands were used each day. That is how I shall write this part. Some of the Commands are going to be omitted. I am only going to writing the really interesting ones down. The rest you can get with your experience with your Service Dog at training camp when you attend it!

I remember the first day it was around 10 and we had finished doing the Commands inside of the classroom. We were instructed to take the dogs outside to walk and to go to the bathroom. There was a ramp that went outside of the front door and down the front of the building to the road below. There was no traffic on the road, it was for students only. I took Paige down the walkway to the corner of the building and told her to "Better Go Now", which was the command to go to the bathroom.

She hesitated at first for about a minute. I only told her once and gave her time to think about it. Then I told her again. And the second time she moved her head back and forth, still thinking. Then the third time she went pee. I got it in my head from that that she had to think through the Commands to be able to act on them, so there needed to be a pause between the time I gave the first Command and the time that I followed up on it. I had gotten that concept mostly from the Commands that I had given to her from the list of commands in the CSTADPTM.

For the Commands list for the first day I started by calling her name to get her used to it. She responded by wagging her ears from side-to-side and raising her paw for a handshake. That was so good of her. Then I told her to "Sit!" and waved my palm upwards as one is supposed to do when giving that Command. She immediately sat down with her front paws out and her rear paws laying underneath with her ears wagging. She wagged her ears to show that she was getting the Command and doing the action required… which included wagging the ears.

Then I told her "Down!" and waved my palm downwards from my head to my waist. She lay down and put her head down on the ground. That was a very active dog, relaxing as such. I was giving her a treat every time she followed a Command and performed it with action along those lines, and she really enjoyed them. The treats had been given to me by the instructors who had used them as a demonstration of treats to their Service Dogs when teaching us the lesson on Commands. That was really nice of them and it gave us the know-how of how to give our Dogs the treats they deserved. And it worked miraculously!

There were other Commands that we put out on the first day. It is hard for me to look at the list of Commands in the CSTADPTM at the same time as using my computer, so I am just going to tell you about the ones I remember from memory. That is not all of them. You will learn them when you get the book and go to class on them.

2nd Day of Commands: The Commands started with us walking to a door that led from the classroom to the outside and standing there with the dog, stationary. The dog was stationary as well, waiting for a Command. Then the handler was to give them the Command "Go Through" and begin to step through the door. The dog listened to the Command and followed out the door to the outside and walked down the walkway to the driveway. Then they were told the Command "Back", which led them to reverse the Go Through movement. There were other Commands on the list for that day, but I don't remember using them.

Then we went into the kennel near their cages. Their names were on their individual cages. There were doors to them with bands of wire on them. We took them in and next to their cage where they slept and told them the Command "Go to Bed", opening the door and letting them in to lay down. They did, and we left them there and the day ended for us. We departed for lunch after asking the instructors questions. There were still the Lessons to follow but without the dog's present, so we came back for those.

3rd Day of Commands: We started by receiving the dogs at the kennel with clothing for them having been given to us by the instructors. The clothing included a collar that had a hole for a leash to be attached to it, which was separate from the vest that the Service Dog wore. The vest had nice stickers on it. One of the stickers said: "Canine Support Teams, Inc. Providers of Assistance Dogs." And a sticker that said: "Please Don't Pet Me... I'm Working". And there was a sticker on the other side that said: "PAWS, For Wounded Veterans" that had a picture of a soldier in uniform waving a solute next to a canine that was standing at attention.

With those items in our possession, the dogs got out of their cages and stood next to us and we told them to "Get Dressed" as we put the equipment on them. They listened. It was simple to put the equipment on. The collar had a noose around a buckle that allowed the handler to loosen its grip when putting it on. The vest was really simple as well. There was a strap that went around the neck of the dog with no buckle that went on by feel, and the other strap went around its waist and had to be attached by unbuckling it at the beginning and putting it into place, then attaching the buckle around the waist to the other side. It was really easy.

Then we took the dog to the table outside and sat down on the bench and told her to "Go In". With that Command she would nestle under the table and lay down underneath it, waiting for another Command. Then, because we were outside and it was approaching lunchtime, and we were taking the Dogs for a walk that day, we took the Dogs by the side of the building and told her to "Better Go Now". That was the callsign to Go to The Bathroom. She didn't listen the first couple of times that I told her, then she started to pee. I was drawing the conclusion from the commands that she had to access her memory and use her intelligence to determine what the actions were that she was to take per command, and that took some time. So, her responses were not immediate, as one would expect... but they were accurate, with some thought included in the transaction.

We were told by the instructors to give the command "Quiet" if the Dog was barking unnecessarily. Paige never barked unnecessarily, though, so I didn't give her that command until later. And even then, I would use the

Command "Don't!" to tell her not to bark at all. I should use the command "Quiet", though. Now I will.

There were other Commands for day three, just like the other days. And there will be other Commands for the remaining days that I don't mention in order to save space. Like I have said already, if you want to know the Commands, get yourself a *Canine Support Teams Assistance Dog Program Training Manual* and read it.

I was really emotional when I was giving her the Commands. I would think about the verbiage of what I was about to say and try to say it in terms and genuflection that she would understand readily. I looked at her response and she responded every time, which was nice, and it meant that I was saying the terms correctly. It was a profound experience to have such a positive element on the mindset of my Service Dog, a Dog that had been trained in the elements of Service and companionship. And it was without me having any experience in it. That said a lot about the capabilities of the instructors, Carol and Shara and Debrah. They were such excellent instructors that they taught us about the Commands the very first day and we were able to use them immediately. And the instructors respected that many of us students were military or former military. They had taken part in the process for bringing the Dogs to PAWS for Wounded Veterans. And they also had helped to teach Paige how to handle Post Traumatic Stress Disorder, which I have from 7 Force Reconnaissance Marines drowning on a helicopter doing the same training we had done. Paige licks my hand or leg when I start to have an episode, which calms me right on down. That is such a good thing of her to do. She had learned how to do it in the PAWS program. Overall, my experience with Paige was so outstanding that she has changed my life in many ways to the positive. I can go out in public now without worrying about being murdered because she had been trained to bite and kill any person that threatens to attack me or her for any reason. Granted, there are very few people that she has barked at or moved like she wanted to sic them… but there are a few. I have responded each time with the Command "Leave It!" which is designed to get her to stop whatever action she is attempting to do. And it worked each time. She still moved around back and forth, granted, but she stopped moving towards them like she wanted to bite them. That is so good of her. She knows the Commands well.

That told, now onto Day 4's Commands. We started out in the classroom next to the table, and the instructors gave us each an item to hold. They were somewhat small items, like a folded-up cable for a cellphone or an adapter to an outlet to some microphones or a stick of gum in wrappers. Each of us students then received the instructions on the TV that said multiple commands in the order that we were to give them, for the most part. Next to each instruction was a description of what it was for.

That list of instructions started with the Command "Look"… which was to tell the dog to look at a designated item. Then it was followed by "That's It"... which could be said for any of the following commands if the dog does it and follows it appropriately. That was followed by the command "Get It"... which is instruction for the dog to put the item in it's jaw and hold it. That was followed by "Hold" and "Bring It Here", which caused the dog to bring you the object while holding it in his or her jaw. Then it was followed by the Command "Give", which causes the dog to release the item into your grip. Any of those could be led off by the command of "Get The" (name of the object), which would help the dog separate the object you want from a group of objects around it.

All those commands were given to a dog that was around an object that had been given to the student by the instructors individually, one at a time, and the dogs all followed through with it remarkably. Paige had some hesitation between the time she got the command and the time that she actually performed the command because she had a process of Thinking about what was said to her and processing the action to be taken. But she did the exercise on the second command. That got the idea through to her. Not that she needed it. Dogs are really smart. She just needed the time to perform it.

There were other commands, but I will be covering all of them in the following chapters in this book called *Daily Commands to Paige*.

The Day 5 Commands included teaching the dog to know the difference between a light switch and a regular switch. The command for a light was "Light", which indicated that the dog was to push on a button with its nose. That could be replaced by the Command "Switch", which indicated that the dog was to push on a button with its paw. There were other formats of those commands.

There was also some instruction on Commands for those in wheelchairs, although only a few of the students were in them. They were multiples of the "Pull (Left, Right, Easy, Stop, etcetera). The students didn't really use them if they were not in wheelchairs, because the dogs that had been situated to them may not have been designated as "Pulling Dogs", so they didn't know how to respond to the Commands. The students that were on wheelchairs DID have Pulling Dogs established for them, so they DID give the Commands and got action off of them.

That concludes the Commands we learned to give to them. The Commands for Day 6 were given to us at the Mall by the instructors, and we tried them out verbally. The remainder of the training occurred at the Mall area. We walked up and down stairs outside the movie theatre on the sidewalk, took the dogs in the elevators to the Starbucks on the second story, led out dogs through the stores there and did tricks with them readily, went through the Commands with the Dogs in the stores there, and then returned to Starbucks after a couple hours of graded exercises. The instructors were determining if we had learned enough about how to handle the Service Dogs that we would be keeping them up to their names.

We were tested on the last day of the week, on a Friday. That was a total of a full 2 weeks-worth of classes on handling the Service Dogs, getting on assigned to us each, testing a new area, and finally getting tested on our handling of them. It was remarkable. I really enjoyed it.

When we were there in the classroom in the morning, we learned how to feed the dogs. We arrived around 7 AM and that was time for the Dogs to eat. We were given dishes and a cannister of food for them to eat in it. We put the cannister into the bowl in the Dog's cage and let it go to town eating it. The dogs were hungry! They ate within 15 minutes and then went into the classroom for the lessons and Commands and training.

During the break time we had time to walk the dogs along the driveway to the parking area. We had to put our dogs on a leash in the classroom. Mine was connected to a vest she wore, or her collar… either one would suffice. The reason was because I was going to get a scooter that I was going to walk her on, and that would connect to her vest only. So, I was getting used to it… and getting Paige used to it as well.

We also learned about how the Dog would offer Personal Protection for the clients of them. They would do things like bark at people who would do something negative to the handler like assault them or do something negative to them. All it required was that the IDEA of it was going through their minds. If such a thing happened the dog would be able to sense it, and they would bark at the culprit and start to move like they wanted to sic them. That would require a statement of "No!" or "Don't!" to persuade them to stop doing it. It worked, usually. I say usually because there was a guy outside of the Coffee Shop on a bicycle that came over to me and raised his hand like he wanted to pat me on the shoulder and Paige interpreted it as an assault and started to move at the guy like she wanted to sic him. And she didn't stop at my commands. That tells me that the guy couldn't get those negative things out of his mind… or he started to think about assaulting my dog! Either way, Paige didn't like it and was getting fully ready to bite the culprit.

Eventually he backed off and left, and when he was gone, she stopped barking. That is a good indicator of her skill in determining the presence of a threat to me or her.

That pretty much sums up what I have to say about this class to get the Service Dog to you, the possible participant of the class yourself. The rest of the story is about my handling of the Service Dog Paige, and whatever else I see as being worth writing about along those lines. I am the proud owner of a Service Dog, and it gives me pleasure to write a story about that remarkable and excellent Dog! I hope this story helps you to get and handle one yourself. Please enjoy!

THE NEXT PERIOD WITH THE SERVICE DOG PAIGE

081819

We went for a walk this morning. My roommate took Forest and I took Paige on a scooter that I had gotten for walking her. We went down the street and around a corner and the scooter stopped working! I tried to press the button to get it to go, and the power lights were all on, but it wouldn't steer anywhere. So, I called my roommate and she walked over to move it.

As she arrived a guy came out of the yard, I was next to and asked if we needed help. We said: "that would be nice," and told him that we could show him where we lived, just down the street. He and his partner got a wheel cart and another golf cart to put the scooter into one and drive me in the other back home. My roommate took Paige with her back to the house. When we got to my house the kind guys took the scooter off the wheel cart and put it in our garage where it usually goes. I said "Thank you guys a lot! You are remarkable!" and they went back to their yard. I went into the house with my roommate and kept on thinking about the scooter.

My roommate wanted to take it in and get it fixed, but I saw there was a problem with that. The way that the scooter had a problem was an indicator that there was probably something wrong with the engine. Before, when it ran out of batteries, it would still roll on the tires readily, even with the battery empty. This time, however, the tires would not move at all and the battery was showing that it was full of power. So, that told, there was something wrong with the power to the wheels, I think. I had my roommate check the stuck rear tires when I lifted up the scooter and she found nothing stuck in them. So, that wasn't the problem. The problem was a malfunction in the engine, I think.

I am still writing the previous chapter right now, so I shall get back to that now.

082319

I took Paige with me today to the coffee shop. Krishna dropped us off and talked to us on the way there. She was in a good mood, both Krishna and Paige. As I got off the car, however, a woman got out of her car across the parking lot with a dog. It wasn't a Service Dog; I could tell because Paige really likes Service Dogs and won't bark at them... but she immediately started barking at this dog and moving like she wanted to sic it. I told her to "Leave it!" and she stopped, but still was moving back and forth as I walked forwards with her, looking at it. We went inside and ordered a Tea and the lady with the dog brought it right outside of the window next to where I was going to sit and sat down with the dog in plain sight. But Paige didn't bark or anything as I sat down. And she stayed good the whole time we were there. That is so good of her!

I had the snack bag around my waist filled with Pupperoni and gave some to her when she begged me for some by shaking my hand and looking at my snack bag. She knows how to get treats and gets every time she is hungry. That time she was doing it for a reward for not getting uptight over that dog that was outside on the other side of the glass, some 10 feet away. That is appropriate and intelligent of her to do. That shows that she knows about my means and capabilities, she knows that I have certain responses to body movement (like handshaking), that I carried treats on me in my bag (because she was looking at it when she wanted a treat), and overall it shows her intelligence with getting me to support her with something she wants. She can identify what a Pupperoni tastes like and tell me with a smile or ears wagging whether she likes it or not... and she almost always does, because they are tasty treats. They taste like beef and come in sticks that can be cut into eatable portions and given to the Dog. She likes them a lot!

It was altogether a nice trip. Then, when Krishna came to pick us up, Paige lay down in the back of the car with her head down and looked like she was asleep with her eyes open. She does that when she is faking being asleep. She is really good at it.

As for me, I have been putting my brain into Paige's well-being all day long. I have been writing on Page 32 of this document on Paige and how the class to get her transpired. I am reading over the Canine Support Teams Assistant Dog Instruction Manual and reading over the Lessons we got for the first 5 days there for them. The Lessons are intense and cover a lot, but the words are not too big to understand, and the sentences are precise and accurate. The instruction manual is 100 pages long, which is too much for me to put in this book, so I have reduced the pages by talking about the training of Paige and my mindset instead of the CSTADIM book. This book is designed to give a person the higher capabilities of going to a Canine Support Teams class and getting their book that-a-ways and studying it for the details of it, and thereby becoming a graduated Service Dog owner! That would be so nice!

082619

Yesterday at 4 pm me and Krishna and Paige went to Newport Beach for a seminar given by Gary Sinise...

the guy who played Captain Dan Taylor in the movie Forrest Gump. It was a remarkable get-together. It was held at the Jewish Bat Yahm Temple. They accept people of multiple religions, so we were included. There were a ton of military folk there, either retired or active duty. Some wore uniforms. Others just hats.

We sat in the back because there were no more seats left up front. The people in the row right in front of us turned out to have Golden Doodle dogs too, a black one and a white one, and one was a puppy raiser and the other was an instructor of the Canine Support Teams classes. She recognized us and said "Hi" to us! And Paige didn't bark at the other dogs or anything. She was very attentive to them and looked like she wanted to play. We stayed sitting down as the session started.

Gary Sinise gave a solid story and played videos of the Veterans he has been in contact with... there are a lot of them... and talked about the Gary Sinise Foundation, which helps Veterans with health problems to deal with them and get treatment that is affordable. Gary Sinise's band the Lieutenant Dan Band earns money for the Veterans to have new homes to live in if they are disabled from their service. He has earned enough for multiple houses.

While he was giving his speech, I took Paige outside to go to the bathroom. She didn't go, so I brought her back inside. On the way back into the auditorium we walked past an aisle that had people seated on either side and had to walk back to my seat next to Krishna. On the way Paige saw another dog and started to bark at it! I told her to "Leave it" and she stopped and walked back with me to where we were sitting down. From there she was a really good dog.

We watched the rest of the session with both Gary Sinise and the owner of the Temple Bat Yahm talking about Gary's experiences with the Veterans. Then they finished and told us to go ahead and go out the doors to the outside and each of us there were to get a copy of Gary Sinise's written book. So we began to walk over there, and on the way saw Shari Butterworth, my instructor from the Canine Support Teams class to get Paige, and Carol Roquemore, the owner of Canine Support Teams who has started that miraculous organization! They had a couple of dogs with them, too. Paige liked them a lot. She wanted to walk right next to them.

We went out and got a couple of books by Gary Sinise and let to get some gas. Krishna pulled out readily. Paige didn't even go to the bathroom except to pee in the grass. She had eaten a whole meal while there at the temple, so we took her outside at the house to go to the bathroom, and she did. We left it for the next day to clean it up. We do that sometimes. It doesn't bother the dog at all.

Then it was late, and we lay down to go to sleep. Paige lay down in the front room and looked like she went to sleep. She had had a really good day out with me and Krishna. And she did an excellent job being a good dog.

082719

I am trying to think of something nice to do with Paige now. I am not using many Commands with her. We have a neighbor named Eve who has a dog named Sadie who is an excellent dog. She has taught it to do a lot of tricks, and it does them because it is its way of earning treats. I want to start to use Commands more for Paige. The reason is because I am tested on them once per year, around March each year, and because she enjoys a reason to get the treats. Right now, I just give her treats when she begs for one, and she begs three times and gets three segments of treats given to her. She likes the Pupperoni, so I give her three slabs of it per time that I give her some. So, that said, it is likely that she will appreciate the challenge of doing the Commands and getting treats for it. That is her nature, and she is a Dog with a really high caliber of nature!

I went to the Coffee Shop today and got some tea and coffee there. Paige was a good dog and just sat at the edge of my chair and let the staff lady pet her repeatedly, saying good things to her. She likes the attention. The staff brought her over some water right away in a dish, like they usually do when I am there, and put it on the ground within reach of her leash and let her start to drink some water.

The staff of the Coffee Shop like Paige a lot. They always come over and pet her when we are there. I think they will like it if I start to do more tricks with her. I shall start to restudy my Commands and give her more of them as time calls it to be appropriate. As it stands right now I am writing the part of this book that you have already read over that talks about the Class I had to get Paige from the Canine Support Teams and that has parts in it about the Commands we used to communicate with the Service Dogs. So, I am not going to write it again. But I am still writing it, and reading over the manual on the class, so I can't start to redo the Commands quite yet. I will tell you about it when I do. That will be a good part of this book… a full rendition of the capabilities of the Service Dog and its caring Handler.

I just talked to Krishna about what I should write in this book about Paige, and she said that I should write about my emotions during actions with Paige and about how she is handled by the other people and her personality and how she interacts with others. I can do that! This is going to make my book a lot more detailed than it was before… and it is probably going to cause me to finish the book long before Paige dies in another 12 years. I should be able to finish the book within a few months, if I am writing it in a format where I am putting a couple pages per day in here. We'll see where it goes. Hopefully Paige lives until she is at least 18 years old… just like Forest, our other dog, is right now!

I shall also write about Paige's intelligence, and I will be asking her questions about physics and writing down what her answers are. When I asked her the other day if she understood Einstein's Theory of Relativity, she immediately raised up her paw to shake my hand. That is a sign of high intelligence! I shall see over time what her answers are to those questions. But first I am going to read the book written by Gary Sinise called *Grateful American: A Journey from Self to Service*. It is a very excellently written book. It talks a lot about the Veterans of the USA. Solid!

082819

I am in the house now in the little side room that is used by Mo and the door is shut and Paige is standing next to me on the bed wanting to leave this tiny room. The maintenance guys are out in the bathrooms and had been installing different toilets and tiles. They are done installing the tiles, which look really nice, but they ran into a problem with the toilet. Above the old toilet there was a shelf extending over it, and the new toilet is too tall to fit underneath it! Horrible! So, Krishna went back to the store to see if she could get one that was smaller. She had told them about the issue when she had gotten the toilets in the first place, but they didn't listen to her and give her one the right size. Fools.

So, Krishna returned with a toilet that was the right size and lunch in the shape of tacos and burritos for us. Then they ate and got back to work. I went back into the room that had Paige and Forest in it. Paige immediately came over to me and put her head on my leg like she wanted to leave. Eventually, Krishna took Paige and Forest out of the room and let them run around in the front room for a spell. Krishna eventually brought Paige back to the room and told her "look, there he is (me), he hasn't gone anywhere! See!" and with that Krishna left but left the door open. Paige left soon after and I haven't seen her again yet.

I have been feeling moderate emotion around Paige today. Initially, we went to the Coffee Shop really early because we had to be here before the maintenance people showed up… so I was only there for an hour. Paige got pet by the waitress there that has 6 different Bulldogs of her own and she really likes dogs. Paige enjoys getting pet by her immensely, and she sniffs the waitress's gown for smells of the other dogs. She smiles and seems to like it! No other customers came over to Paige that morning, though. The place hardly had anyone in there, anyways.

I really enjoy Paige's good foundation when she is getting pet. I like it too when she sniffs other owners of dogs to smell the dogs in their uniforms and clothes. She is such an intelligent dog. It makes sense that I would like it when things are going well for her because that is also what makes her happy.

Then we went home with no incident and Paige sat in the back of the car silent and happy. She didn't bark at any of the dogs that were walking on the sidewalk next to the car. Then we got home, and she didn't even beg me for a treat while waiting for the maintenance men to come over. When they arrived me and Krishna had lay down plastic fibers over the floor to protect it from the maintenance men getting fibers and junk on the floors. Paige was really good and didn't stand on them or disrupt them in any way. And she sat out of the way for the maintenance guys to walk by without stepping on her tail or paws. That was really thoughtful of her, to think of the motion of the other species and to put her body out of the way of movement of that species. So thoughtful...

Eventually, Krishna put Paige and Forest into the side room and shut the door. I eventually went in there and watched some TV or read my book or wrote on my computer. Now the maintenance men are about done with the toilets. One of them is getting to take my nice bicycle for free, since I can't ride it anymore, I decided to give it to him. He thanked me and said many nice things to me. He deserves it. He is an excellent and kind guy. And they did outstanding work on the toilets! Ok, they are done with the toilets now and mine looks outstanding. I am so pleased today you cannot imagine. But then again, perhaps you can if your imagination is good!

That is all I have to say about Paige for today. It's time for her dinner. I will get it for her then let her rest some more.

082919

Today this morning I took Paige to the Coffee Shop and had some coffee there for two hours. She was pet by the staff there. There are two new owners to the place. They have come up and said Hi to me and Paige. They like her and have no problems with me bringing her in there. She is a Service Dog, after all, and they know that because I told them. They probably guessed it anyways. It seemed like they did from their response to my output. They are such nice owners. They are doing a lot to enhance the Coffee Shop. They brought in flowers in vases and put them around, they brought in a new big table and put it in there, some small tables have been added and the tables in there remodeled and put in other places, they painted the men's bathroom and changed the lights in there to be brighter and more colorful, and they changed the lights over the counter where the coffees and teas and smoothies are bought. They even added some drinks to the drink menu and so far have erased one of their drink menus on the wall for replacement with a new menu… which hasn't been done quite yet because they are still putting out samples of drinks to see what to put on there. But overall, they are doing a lot to improve the place. It is getting a lot more customers nowadays and is a lot busier. Remarkable!

Paige was calm when we were in there. I asked her if she wanted to go to the Coffee Shop on the way there and she immediately put her tongue on her teeth and wagged it from side to side, like she was giving me a response to the question in doggy-speak. What a happy dog! So, I walked her in pleased and asked the waitresses to bring

Paige a dish of water for her, my Service Dog, and they said "Ok!" and did so shortly after.

Paige even begged me for a treat a couple times, and I gave her a double slab serving each time. They are special treats that I have in her pouch right now, so it is acceptable that I give her less than the Pupperoni. Once her treats were finished and she was done eating them, she lay down and put her head down and looked at the waitresses, waiting for the one with the 6 Bulldogs to come over and pet her. But there were a lot of customers there, so she didn't until later. That was okay. Paige just lay there, relaxing and learning about waitressing.

I am sure that if her paws did what human hands could do then she would stand up and waitress for the customers herself! The Dog is a Genius! I shall start to talk to her about science and Particle Physics and Quantum Theory and Relativity Theory as soon as I am done writing the chapter before this chapter. I am still writing it, so you are going to have to wait, since I am writing both of these chapters at the same time! Interesting, isn't it?

What's not interesting... well, in some ways, it ISN'T interesting I think... is the fact that Paige was seen as having diarrhea last night. We had gone to Black Angus for some steaks and Krishna had given Paige half of her steak there. Then she got diarrhea. That is too bad. We are certain it was from the food at the restaurant. So, I didn't feed her any of her food last night, and she went out for more diarrhea today. She is doing okay now, I think. She has pooped enough.

Break time for me. It is starting to come to my conclusion that I am going to only write a book for the next year about Paige, then I will have a full book-length story done. That is okay. Knowing that is going to change the items of my stories that I write about. I think I will be able to fill a lot of the book with chapters about how I am responding to Paige's intelligence and asking her questions. There will also be a section on the Commands that I give to her when I start to give her a whole host of Commands again. I have to finish reading over the Commands and writing about them before I do that, though. That should be enough to finish the book. I want it to be a nice book for anyone who has or wants to get a Service Dog to have. I think that it is off to a good start!

I keep Paige's food in a cannister in the Pantry, which is the living room and kitchen away from my room in which she eats. She has a dish of metal that she eats out of that has prints of doggy paws and animal faces stamped on the sides of it. I take her dish over to the pantry to the container with the food in it twice per day… once in the morning at 7 am and once at night around 4 pm … to get her food with a one-cup measuring cup each time. She follows me there from the room and listens to me put it in the dish then leads me back to the room to eat. She gets so excited to see it… she smiles and wags her ears! She eats Blue Mountain Dog Food, which is the healthiest brand we could find. We get it from Chewy Petfood at a really good price. I highly recommend them. They deliver as needed and bill your credit card.

Paige is a big Dog. She is a Golden Doodle, which is a Golden Retriever mixed with a Poodle. Both of those kinds of dogs can be really big when they are giving birth, and Paige had two big parents, so she is a Big Dog. She weighs about 95 pounds! That is big! And she has a big head and big paws, too.

She doesn't shed hardly at all, and she is hypoallergenic. That means that she does not cause allergies and is nice and easy to clean up on. She is also easy to groom. I spend the average amount to get her groomed, but she doesn't take as long as the usual dog. She is such a delightful dog!

090119

I took Paige with me to the Coffee Shop today. I have already said it has two new owners, and today they had an Opening Party there. It was so nice! I walked in there and saw that there were a lot of customers there for the party, but there was an open seat at the table that I usually sit at and the other seat was taken by a waiter that works there that is a friend of mine. The female owner said "Hi" to me and said that there was a worker sitting at the table and I would be able to sit there. That was nice of her. She told me yesterday that the owners had saved a place there for me to sit, since I was a regular customer. I told her that it was nice of them to do and thanked her. Then the waiter got up and I sat down.

There were a couple elderly people sitting on the couch next to my table. He offered me a seat and I told him that I was okay. Then they began to talk to me. They asked me questions about my Service Dog. I told them that she WAS a Service Dog and had been highly trained and had a high mental capability. "She is intelligent", I told them. They asked me about her training, and I told them about the class I took to get her, and the grant that I had subscribed to. They listened, and then saw my Recon hat and asked about my military service. I told them that I had been in Snipers, then Force Reconnaissance Company… which is a branch of Special Forces… and it was an excellent time. They liked my story.

Then I began to type, since about an hour and a half had passed in those couple's time. There was only about 30 minutes left. As I typed the end of the previous chapter in this book the new owners got up in front of the people there at the Coffee Shop and started to say all kinds of nice things about the people and their staff. Then the male owner said my name and said I was an author and that I came there a lot and told me to wave at the crowd. I did, and they clapped and cheered!

Then my ride showed up. Paige was done getting treats by that time, so we got in the car and went to the Sushi place for me to get dinner. I had 3 Piece Sashimi there, and it was delicious. Paige sat under the table all hungry and ready to eat her dinner which she did when we got home.

Paige didn't bark at anyone at the Coffee Shop or move like she wanted to sic anyone. That was so nice of her to do! Nobody brought a dog to the outside, so she had nothing to get upset over. That was good of her.

We are home now. She is laying down, resting. Starting tomorrow I am going to take my list of Commands and study them to start to give her more Commands as part of that next chapter of this book that I am going to write.

090419

Today we took a trip about an hour away to the VA Hospital to get my medicines and for me to see the psychiatrist that handles my medicines and does a study of my mental state. I told him all sorts of good things about me, because I have been feeling really good since I have had Paige.

We were waiting to see him in an open area outside the door to the offices where a lot of other patients were waiting for the doctors to call them. I started to move with Paige and my rollator to a bench to sit on behind some people already there. As I moved there, Paige got barked at by a little tiny chihuahua. It immediately obstructed her, and she started to move like she wanted to sic it and she was barking and barking at it! I pulled on her leash and gave her the command of "Don't!" She stopped barking but kept on tugging on the leash. At least she was listening to the command.

As she sat down next to me and my rollator, I took a treat out of my bag and gave it to her, saying the words: "Thank you for listening to me say Don't". I said it in an appreciative tone and not loud, so she wouldn't think my tone of "Don't" was directed to her not eating the treats I was giving her. She was SUPPOSED to eat them!

Overall it was a good trip. I told her "Let's Go" as we were leaving the VA building, and as we were walking in the shadow of the eaves overhead Krishna went over to ask a guy about his Scooter and where he got it fixed at, and at the same time a lady came to me with a Dog in a vest. I was at first worried that Paige would bark at it, but she was very friendly, and at the same time I saw that the dog had a "Service Dog" label stamped to its vest. That was good. It showed me that Paige was interacting with him or her positively because it was a Service Dog... and so is Paige!

We walked back to the car happy as clams. That was an excellent day with Paige.

090619

Today Paige is doing really good. She got up early and I ate my medicine when my alarm went off, then I sat around for an hour until it was time to give Paige some breakfast made out of Blue Wilderness Dog Food. It is healthy, prime, tasty, and delicious! (I haven't eaten any of it myself... it IS Dog food, mind you, but Paige really likes it and comes to nibble on it immediately upon the time it is served! So nice of her to do! I tell her every time I serve it: "Dinner (or Breakfast) is served!" and she comes in and eats it readily. She understands the verbiage!)

To leave the house and go to the Coffee Shop, I told her the command of "Let's Go", and she came right away walking by my rear in my direction. We went out the door and she hesitated on the other side, so I told her "Let's Go" again and she came to the car. She got in readily when I gave her the command of "Car" and she got into the back seat. She knows the difference between the seats, and which one is hers.

As we were driving down the street, we saw our neighbor walking her medium-sized to small dog, which is a friendly and excitable pooch. She is a girl, like Paige, and Paige really likes her. She knows as many tricks as Paige knows, too. Remarkable! Her handler waved at us and said "hi!" and was pleased to see us. We said "Hi, you are walking your fantastic Dog. Fantastic! Have a good day!" And at that we had to drive away. She said: "Thank you!" It was so nice to see her and her Dog, I thought they were miraculous.

Paige came with me to the Coffee Shop. There was some guy sitting in my seat, so I had to push a table out from the wall so there would be room for Paige to sit behind it. A lady at the table next to me helped move the chairs out into their position. Then I sat down, and Paige lay down on the interior spot behind the table between the table and the window leading to the outside. She was calm and peaceful. What a good Dog! I have been typing on my computer ever since getting here, after I got a drink, and Paige has been laying next to the table all happy to be here. She got some water in a dish from the waitress and drank some of it, but she wasn't pet by her. She can't be pet anymore… we had a new sticker woven into her vest that says "Please Don't Pet Me… I'm Working". That was a sticker that we had gotten from the Canine Support Teams and during my instruction with them they had told me that nobody was supposed to pet the Dog because the Dog was protecting its handler and them petting it would confuse it if they did something negative like assault the handler or the Service Dog. So, no petting was allowed.

Overall, Paige is doing really good today. I am going to read some more of the second day of Commands to give to her today, and I will give them to her later today, or tomorrow, and see how she does. The Commands are not regular Commands… they are abbreviated by the conditions in which they are given… so it may not go through unless there is a skinny space to move through. I don't know where one of those is. I would have to put out chairs to make on like that, I think, and even that would seem irregular to the Dog. So, I may not be able to give her certain Commands. We'll see.

I shall write about it in my Commands chapter of this book. See, the book is separated by subject matter. There is a lot to write about regarding Paige! So, it is!

See ya!

090819

I am at the Coffee Shop with Paige. She is calm and happy. I have gotten a treat for myself from the counter and she wanted some of it. It was a Protein Bar made out of hazelnuts and cashews and dates and dark chocolate. Paige couldn't have any of that because I didn't know if it was digestible by her, so I gave her some Pupperoni and some Beef Bits as a snack. She was hungry and ate a lot of them! Then, when she was done, she lay down and put her head down and rested. I began to write about it.

I haven't gone through day 2 of the CSTADPTM Commands with Paige yet. There are commands that are for narrow passageways and to get the dog to walk backwards through them... but I don't know where such a passageway is. The only thing I can think of like that around here is the Elevator at the Mall. But I don't want to have to have Paige walk backwards through the elevator door incase it starts to close on her. That would be horrible! So, I probably will just try to get her to do it through the house or the garage where the Van is parked and there is a narrow corridor between the Van and the chair and scooter in the garage.

Either way, I have to get those commands out. I will be tested on them in about 6 months by the Canine Support Team Staff. Paige and I both will be tested on them at the Mall, if they do it at the same place that they have done it for the last two years. I was tested there at the Mall in March 2017 for the class I had to get Paige, and I passed it. Then I was tested again in 2018, around March then too, and I passed. There were some issues with the commands I gave in the second term, though. I worked on them, but I have forgotten what they were. I know that I haven't really been giving my Dog Service Commands much. It is difficult for me to remember, and she does things like "Let's Go" or "Come Here" without me saying any Commands of that nature... she just DOES it! She is a really intelligent Dog, but I am worried that she will have forgotten some of the Commands that I was giving her during the Class. Granted, it had only been a year since she got them... but a year is a long darn time!

Paige likes to come to the Coffee Shop with me. A waitress that has 6 different Pit Bulls came over today and tried to pet Paige. I told her that Paige had a new sticker on her vest that said "Please Don't Pet Me... I'm Working". She apologized and asked me if that was a Service Dog thing, I put on there. I told her it was, that the Service Dog was not supposed to be pet by anyone because that person could assault me, or the Dog and it would be confused if they were petting her. The waitress said that was okay but that she wouldn't assault me or anything like that. I said that was good, but the Service Dog had to be treated the same by everybody.

It is a tall order to have a Service Dog. They take up a lot of attention. But I like it. Paige is a remarkable animal. She knows hand and arm signals and knows how to bark at things she doesn't like and play with Forest. She shakes my hand when she wants a treat attached to the response. She also shakes hands to say the word "Yes!" to the questions I ask of her. And she understands the elements of science. I am writing a chapter in this book about the scientific questions I ask of her. In it I am going to put the elements of the question of: "What sign do you give me that means a "Yes?" How about a "No?"" It shall be an elegant chapter with a lot of foresight into the elements of the story so that the reader will understand what it was that I saw as a response to my questions and the answers as put forth by Paige.

That about concludes my time at the Coffee Shop today. I shall be reading about the Commands when I get home today, and probably give Paige some to see how she does. It is going on 3:30 pm right now, so it might be a little late for me to attempt Commands with her. I don't know. I will try, though.

Actually, I will try tomorrow morning when I know she is awake.

090919

I tried the commands of "Go Through" and "Back" in the garage, and Paige did them somewhat... it was clear to me that her memory was struggling with the memory of what the body position for them was and what they mean... but she DID walk backwards for part of the issue. She wanted to walk forwards, though. I guess it wasn't narrow enough to make her want to walk backwards. Hmm. I will continue to work on her with those commands there until she starts to follow them readily. That is the only place that I know of with a narrow corridor that we go to on a regular basis, so it MUST work!

I am reading the Day 3 Commands right now, and there are some commands that I don't remember ever using with Paige. Commands like "Speak", which is designed to get the Dog to start to bark on command for communication with an individual, or "Quiet", which is designed to stop the Dog from barking... those are two commands which I have no memory of ever using. I have always used the command "Don't" to stop the Dog from barking and had never used the command "Speak". I had tried to use a command I made up called "Bark", but nothing came of it. There was no barking.

I shall try the Command of "Speak" and "Quiet" over the course of the next couple of days. We are going to be at the cabin in the mountains for the next 4 days, so the Dog may be distracted. We'll see when I try the Commands out later!

091319

I didn't try any Commands at the cabin. We are back down in town now, at home. I am at the Coffee Shop right now with Paige. A really nice lady came over and asked if she could pet Paige... but I told her that she was wearing a sticker that said: "Please Don't Pet Me". So, the lady said "Ok" and asked what Paige's name was. I told her what her name was... "Paige... like a book page!" and she liked it. She asked what kind of dog Paige was, and I told her she was a Golden Doodle.

"That is like a Golden Retriever and a Poodle mixed together," I said. "Either breed can be a really large dog as a parent, and BOTH of Paige's parents were big dogs. Thus, Paige is a huge dog in and of herself!"

The lady liked that. She asked me what it was that Paige could do. "She is an excellent Dog... I can tell. And she is a Service Dog, that is what her sticker says. What services does she do for you?"

"Oh, she does a lot. Service Dogs are trained to handle mental disabilities and things like that. Things the average person can't think of. I have PTSD from the military. Paige knows how to handle it. When I start to have an episode, she will come up to me and start to lick my arm or leg or try to shake my hand and it calms me down immediately! It is so nice to be around her! She knows how to do things like that. She was trained by PAWS. That is a service for Service Dogs to be trained in handling Disabled Veterans. Thus, she knows from that how to handle PTSD. She probably also knows how to handle Obsessive Compulsive Disorder and other ones I don't know about. I know about PTSD because I have it. But she helps a lot with it! I rarely have an episode anymore because of her."

"That is so nice," the lady said. "How long have you had her?"

"I have had her for 2 ½ years now. Do you want to hear how I got her?"

"Yes, I do. I do!"

"I applied for a grant through the Canine Support Teams Assistance Dog Trainers about 4 ½ years ago. They used the grant money to give birth to Paige and they began to train her to be a Service Dog for 2 years. Then they put me through a 2-week course to learn how to give her Commands and to raise her and be raised BY her and they tested me, and I passed the course and got her as her handler! I have had her with me everywhere ever since! Nice, huh?"

"That is very nice! Where did you serve in the military?" She was really listening to the conversation and drawing conclusions from the fact that I had told her about the PTSD and the military.

"I was in the Marine Corps. I started out as a Sniper for 4 years. Then I transferred over to Force Reconnaissance Company, which is a Special Forces unit in the USMC."

"Yeah, they are Special Forces. Good! Was that a challenge?"

"It was very challenging. I was only there for 4 years. That is the normal time that people are there for their first term because it is so challenging that physically arduous that it drives them to go somewhere else after their 4-year term is up. I stayed in the Marines after and went to the Mountain Warfare Training Center to train people how to rock climb and mountain climb and fight in mountains to train them to go to Afghanistan. I trained a lot of Special Forces and Recon Marines there. But then I had to get out of the Marines after I had been in the military for 11 years because I had been injured in Force Recon in the parachute course and was still injured from it 4 years later. Because of that injury I was not going to be able to go back into Force Recon and would have had to go to Headquarters. That would have been a loss in rank for me. So, I decided to get out."

"That's too bad. But you have a wonderful Dog with you now! You are an excellent Dog, Paige! Glad you take good care of your Master!" The lady really liked the conversation. "Thank you so much for serving for us! It means so much! Nice to meet you and Paige! Take it easy, Paige! And what is your name?"

"My name is Jason. And yours is...?"

"Secret. My name is Secret. Take it easy. Good conversation with you!" She went and sat down. I sat down and began to write this part of the story.

My ride would be here in 45 minutes. I am reading over Day 3 Commands for Paige from the CSTADPTM. It is my hope that I will be able to give her the Commands over the next couple of days. Some of the commands I have never given her, so I don't even know if they will work. But she was trained in her commands to a degree from the program PAWS for Wounded Veterans, so she probably has been trained in those commands. She probably has received the "Speak" command, which is to bark at someone, or the "Quiet" command, which is to stop barking. She probably had been trained in those. The instructors of the course I was in probably didn't think it was necessary to tell me to give her those commands. But they had the same list as I did. I got my list from them at the beginning of the course. So... I don't know what's up. I am going to study the Commands for each day and give them to her, over time.

And I will write down the outcome in the Commands chapter of this book.

That is all for now. I shall write more in this chapter later.

091819

I haven't said anything about it yet, but in 2013 I was the victim of vehicular homicide. I just got word from my attorney that there are laws against us, and he wants to settle. So, I said "ok" and am waiting for him to call us with information on the very low sum of money that he'll be getting for it. In the process, I have started to look at getting my books I have written published and to interview the publishers. I will be asking Paige questions about it as time progresses. It is disruptive to my mind thinking that we may lose the trial to a VA that is totally corrupt... and it is CORRUPT... but there is nothing I can do about it. I can only hope that I can get published for free. My roommate is going to call the publisher that we talked to last year on the phone in the morning and see if she wants to read over my book and determine the publishing calls. I hope it happens. There is another lady that asked me to send a query and 3 pages of the book for her to review and I sent it to her. I haven't gotten a response back yet... I will within the next three weeks. That is the time limit. We'll see.

I'm going to write in my chapter about my conversation with Paige about science about how I am going to also talk to her about my writing. I am also going to include my health and the disability benefits I am trying to get for the PTSD that I got from the military. The PTSD had severe consequences. It created head trauma that lasted for from 2005 to 2016... nearly 11 years of it. That is a lot of time. I am going to ask Paige questions about it and my disability and get her input on the matters I ask her about. I will be paying attention to the subtle points of her conversation: how she waggles her ears, where she moves her head, how she crouches with her hind legs, what she does with her chin and jaw, all those things will be taken into account. Other things I haven't thought of yet, too! I shall write about them all here in the Chapter on *Conversation with Paige About Science.*

Me and Paige went to the Coffee Shop today and there was a lady there that was standing in glasses and Paige went over to her and began to sniff her leg a lot. The lady was kind and nice and said: "Well look at her! She can smell my other dogs! I have a *lot* of them!" She was all cheer-filled. Then she asked of me: "Can I pet your Dog?"

I replied what her sticker said and showed it to her. She said "Ok" and kept her hands from petting Paige. I told her that Paige was a Service Dog the way her sticker says and that she knows all kinds of tricks.

"She plays with our other Dog, who is a Burmese Mountain Dog and Border Collie mix," I told her. She smiled.

"That is an excellent Dog! What kind of Dog is she? A Labra-Doodle?"

"No, she is a Golden Doodle. A smart and kind Dog, she is. She really likes our other Dog!"

"Oh, that is so nice! Look at her smelling my leg!"

"Ok, gotta get a drink now. Nice to meet you, miss!"

"Nice to meet you, sir! And your Dog too!" She was so kind. She went on her way and I went to the counter to get a drink.

Then she left and Paige and I went and sat down. Paige is laying down now, looking in her Sleep Mode.

Paige is going crazy over the rats in the attic.

She goes into the kitchen today and starts to move her head really rapidly back and forth, her hears down and pacing back and forth. Then her ears come up because she can hear the rats running around up there in the attic and she starts to bark at them. Then I can hear them start to run, pounding on the attic (which is part of our ceiling) and making a bunch of noise towards my room. Paige barks and barks and then, finally, Krishna comes out of her room because she was trying to sleep and yells at Paige: "SHUT UP!" Paige listens to Krishna and stops barking but keeps on wagging her head back and forth. The sound of the rats is gone, though, so Paige stops waggling around.

There was a website that said that Dogs were a severe prevention of rat infestation. They bark at the rats and it scares them wholly... the rats begin to bolt for cover at the barks and they run and run and run out of the house! That is what we need, if we can't find a readily cost-removed trap to stop them from approaching the house in the first place. The Dog can drive them away with her barking... although Krishna doesn't like the barking because it wakes Krishna up. Oh well. There is nothing else we can do at this time for it.

Paige walks around all calm and ready for adventure! She is a peaceful dog with no issues other than the occasional non-Service-Dog that she sees that she knows will bite its owner or another person. She barks and barks at them and moves like she wants to sic them! I keep control of her leash, however, so she doesn't go and cause some trouble. Other owners would get all uptight if Paige went over and bit their dog... even if he or she would go and bite a person or another animal. They don't understand that Dogs are bred and trained to exact learning methods and lessons that they can teach about bad behavior. I know it because I live with a Service Dog that does it! So, I get to see it occurring on a daily basis (somewhat).

Paige came over when I was making lunch in the microwave and lay down next to the door. She wants to go outside. I know this because of her behaviors. But she doesn't have to go to the bathroom. She hasn't eaten yet. She just wants to sit out there. But it is too hot for her, I think. It is 100 degrees out there. Too hot. So, I kept her inside. She is okay in here. She lay down with her head up, looking at me. She looked like she was smiling. Perhaps she was! I like that Dog a lot. I love her. She is such a wonderful creature and animal that she is a remarkable addition to my life. The instructors of the Canine Support Teams knew that when they gave her to me to train. They did such an excellent job of it! I only hope that I am able to keep up with the training and the Commands with her. I haven't gone over many of the

Commands lately. I am still on Day 3... and there are 10 days in the book. Horrible! I shall continue tomorrow.

As it stands, I am writing a lot of books right now, and I am working on getting the books I have already written published. There is a lot to getting edited and published. And I have to re-read over the books to change the names of people I don't want to sue me for putting them in a book, too. Bad people are in the books. But it has been a while since I have read over them, so I don't remember all the names of the people that I shouldn't have named in them... so I am going to have to read over them in Microsoft Word and change the names therein. It can be done. It is just going to take some time.

That is all I have to write here. Now onto writing in the other books! (Or watching TV.)

Oh man. Forest has an ear infection.

Krishna went over to him yesterday and put her hand on his ear to pet him, and he yelped out loud in pain! She didn't do it hard or anything! Well, I went over to him later and asked her the question: "Did you look at his ears?" to see if there was anything wrong with them.

"Oh, that is a good idea!" she said. "Do it!"

So, I did, and there was foam and bruising inside his ear. It looked like it was infected. She saw it and got alarmed. "Oh man, I am going to take him into the veterinarians!" She got on the phone and called the animal hospital in our town about him and scheduled an appointment to be seen by the staff.

I am at the Coffee Shop right now. We went there to drop me and my Service Dog off before the appointment with the doctor for Forest is supposed to go. I hope he is okay. He is 19 years old right now, which is about 4 years past the time he was supposed to die, so it may be time for the doctors to put him down. He could have cancer or a tumor or brain damage. There is no way for us civilians to tell without diagnosis equipment and the know-how of how to use it. But I hope that Forest is okay and lives. I like him a lot.

And Paige will be lonely when he dies. So, I hope he doesn't die. But it is time to, so I understand.

I am thinking about what it must be like to be "put down" by a doctor. That would involve getting a shot of a substance. The substance would intercede perhaps with the brain and stop it from sending signals to the body. It would probably also stop the heart from beating my removing the pulse from the nerves that go to it. How that happens is a mystery to me, but I a sure that such a thing happens. Either that or the brain cells stop functioning and they stop the workings of the body, so it dies.

Either way, I hope it is painless, because Forest is going to be with me in the Hereafter after I die, with Paige and Krishna, and we will all be together there in holiness and happiness and pleasant being. Thus, I want Forest to be happy and painless in his death, so that there is no obstruction to his happiness in the Hereafter.

I shall write more about Forest after the appointment goes. It will be at 2:00 PM today. I hope it goes okay. But he may die. I am aware of that. I will write about it either way... alive and happy or dead.

I shall continue this part in the Chapter called *Paige's Health*.

Today, this morning, it is the second of January, and we were on our way to the Coffee Shop... me and Krishna and Paige. Outside the car was a large dog walking with its owner. Forest was in the car with Paige. Forest saw the dog walking and didn't like it and started to bark and bark and bark a lot at it. Then Paige followed suit and started to bark as well. Paige went beyond that and she raised her paws up on the window and started to bat around at it. Horrible! I turned around in my seat and raised my voice at her, yelling "Don't! Stop it!" at her to council her. She eventually listened... after we had departed the distance between us, and the other dog and it was out of sight.

Paige was calm at the Coffee Shop. There, there was a lady with a little girl standing there who was about two years old that wanted to pet Paige. I told the lady that she was wearing a sticker that said "Please Don't Pet Me... I'm Working". The lady said "Ok, she's a Working Dog" and told her girl not to pet Paige. The girl didn't listen at first and went up and tried to pet Paige. Her mom let her, then told her to stop doing it because Paige was a

Working Dog. Of course, the little girl was too young to understand what her mother meant by the term she was using, so the little girl kept on trying to go over to Paige to pet her some more. She had the petting down for a young girl! Her mother put her hands down and restrained her little girl from petting Paige, and Paige and I departed to the table.

Then the lady and her girl left the building and two other ladies with two little girls who were about three years old each came in. The two girls came over to me and asked me: "Can we pet your Dog?"

I told them the sticker that she had on her. The girl's mother said to her: "Oh, look… she's a Working Dog. You aren't supposed to pet her! Sorry!" She was such a nice lady. She said it in a really positive and readily available fashion. The girls listened to her and said they were sorry and went to go get some coffee. After all, that is what they were here for!

I thanked the lady and told her that she was correct, and that Paige was a Service Dog and that those were not supposed to be pet by other people. "She's a Protective Dog, and if she came into being pet by a stranger and the stranger then hit her or assaulted her or me, then she wouldn't know what to do. It would confuse her. So, to avoid that misunderstanding, there is a ban on her being pet by strangers. Sorry! But thank you for understanding that she is a Working Dog and not petting her! That was nice of you to ask, though! Thank you!" I wanted to explain the circumstances so that they would understand why they may receive the same response from someone else that had a Service Dog that told them the same thing.

They got some coffee and sat down at a table on the other side of the restaurant. They didn't ask to pet Paige again. They understood the message. Then, about 15 minutes later, they left.

Paige was laying down attached to me by the leash with her water dish under the chair next to her. My rollator was stationed next to the table, which had my backpack and the computer out on it. There was a drink container upon the table. Paige was super calm. She was laying so that her head was facing outwards so that she could see the inside of the Coffee Shop, because that was how she protected me from angry strangers. She very rarely finds someone to bark at, though. I am usually treated very well by others. Especially at the Coffee Shop. That is Good for Paige. She doesn't have to worry about getting an interrupted mindset and she gets to keep a positive one that allows her to rest and lay down and look at kind and happy things in the environment!

It is easy to write on the computer in Paige's presence. She usually lays down and keeps her head down and looks forwards. She moves her eyes back and forth so that she can see things to the sides. I have looked at her eyes while she is laying down and gotten a summary of what their effects are. She is a very alert Dog. She pays a lot of attention to her surroundings, and she makes it look like she is asleep, when she is NOT. That is such a good thing of her to do, you cannot imagine a ready difference in the makings of such a reaction! Or can you? I don't know… but it seems like it defies comprehension!

Let me conclude this chapter here. Paige is a remarkable Dog! She is obedient, well- versed, follows Commands well (at least the ones she has been trained in. Some of the Commands on the list of Commands she doesn't know because nobody has trained her in what to do when she gets them) and gets along well with other Service Dogs. She doesn't get along well with regular dogs that aren't Service Dogs because they haven't been trained to do tricks or receive treats for Good Conduct or anything like that that Service Dogs learn to do. So, she doesn't like regular dogs much. She barks at them and moves like she wants to sic them. I keep control of her by Commands and pulling on her leash to apply friction to her collar. Not much. Just enough to tell her to stop her action of barking and the sic.

But overall she is a well obedient Dog. And her capabilities are miraculous. The class that the Canine Support Teams put me through in order to become her handler were miraculous and well organized. I was glad to be there for it. And the capabilities that the class gave to me to be Paige's handler, to be reinforced by the yearly test to continue to handle her, are well performed and well thought out by the Canine Support Teams trainers. They did a miraculous job of training Paige to be a Service Dog, and I definitely appreciate them.

The Canine Support Teams even let us come by in December to give them presents for being great Service Dog trainers! We brought them presents this year and the lady there said that they would even babysit the Dogs when we travelled, and they would groom them there at our request for a small fee. So, we ordered for Paige to get groomed and they did it the next day with remarkable success! They did an excellent job of it, and we thanked them for it. So, Canine Support Teams goes far above and beyond the duties required as the trainers of the Dogs. And they even from them for less than it costs at the pet store to do the same thing. Nice!

So, our capabilities to take care of Paige are helped out by the people who initially trained her to be a Service Dog. And she gets a lot of attention from the people that are out in the areas that I go to with her. They all want to pet her, even though she is wearing a sticker that says that it is not allowed. They listen to my commands to them and to her. They appreciate that she is a Service Dog and a Working Dog. That is so nice of them! And it is very nice that I am able to take her to all the places that I go to, except the Hospital. I understand why there are restrictions on the Hospital, though. If I am getting surgery or a shot or am dying, then she would get upset over that and activate herself really negatively. That is not acceptable, so the hospitals refuse to help people that have a Service Dog present. I understand the reason for that reasoning. So, it is okay. She is allowed to go everywhere else with me. To the Coffee Shop (they like her there and know her by name), to restaurants, on the airplane, on ships to this country, on the train, you name it, she is allowed to go there as long as it is not the hospital.

Things are going really well for Paige. I think that she sees me as a great handler of a Service Dog. I try to do the best for her. And writing this book is helpful, too. It helps me pay attention to what I am doing for her welfare and it helps me to continue to do it at the best of my ability. That is so nice of the ability to write books. I am glad I am an author. And I am glad that Paige helps me to write by keeping my company and giving me the upper hand approval as I continue to write about her and other things within my lifetime. The books that I write about are well-spoken and well spelled, I think. I hope you enjoy them. Paige likes them! I even read to her sometimes! And she likes it a LOT!

Take it easy and read on!

DAILY COMMANDS TO PAIGE

To give Paige adequate Commands I am going to use the manuals that are attached to the Canine Support Teams Assistance Dog Program Training Manual (CSTADPTM) to give me a full rendition of the Commands, rather than go with the abbreviated and single-line filled out version that I have for myself. I will be keeping both versions.

Here, in this section of the book on Paige, I will write down what was done to prepare her for the Command, what I did to prepare Myself to give the Command, the Command I have given verbally with the hand and arm signal if necessary next to it, the length of time between the Command and the reaction by Paige, secondary tries (if necessary), and her reward and what it is when she puts the Command into action.

Now, onto the steps for the Commands...

The primary preparation that I am going to do for her is to have her to "Sit", and thus be prepared to do something. Most of the Commands are a movement from a Sit position anyways. So, that is what I am going to try to do. It is going to be a verbal command, and hopefully after some time doing it passes, she will start to do it on her own without being told to do it. She will come to anticipate when I am preparing to give her Commands and act in respect to that. Not action to the Commands... action to Sit before the Commands are given. That is what I want and will be trying to install in Paige.

Before the issuance of a Command to Paige I am going to think about the things that I must say, before, during, and after the Command to make it plentiful for us. For each Command I will do something with my hand or voice to draw her into doing the object. The tone of my voice during the command will be Happy and Nice and when I tell her something like "My Lap" ... which is designed for her to put her paw on my lap... I will pat my lap with my hand a couple times to get her the idea of "Come into contact with it" ... so she will go and have the desire to put her paws on it. I will watch her after giving her the Command and see when she finishes doing it, then I will say to her "Shake Hands!" and put out my hand for her to shake with her paw. She does that for treats, and I will have them ready to give to her and give her one or two after the Command is over... as a reward for doing it. That will make her very happy and fully ready to do the next trick or Command as called for.

That is, unless she is tired or full of food... then she will likely become resistant to doing more Commands and hesitate too much between the time of the Command and the time of performing the action. Then it is time to Stop giving her Commands and to let her rest.

Other Commands involved the handler doing something with an object or showing the dog what to do. For example, when giving the Command of "Down" it is followed at the same time with the handler pushing his or her hand downwards... which is the body movement for the dog to lay on it's belly by bending its legs down. "Sit" is done at the same time as the opposite hand motion... the hand with palm raised up and moving the hand upwards, a reflection of the dog's legs to its torso. That goes through the animal's head of what to do to make it happen, and it takes the according action to make it occur. I must come up with some kind of movement of my hands for every Command, I think. Some would involve hand-and-arm motions. Others would involve steps and movement. Others would involve distinct commands and tone of voice. I am going to read over my Commands list and determine which one of those it is that I want to use. I will put the methods down in my Commands list below and make it plain to the reader what I am doing for giving the Commands.

That concludes the list of what steps I will be taking to issue the Commands. Now, I shall go into the Commands given and the Service Dog's performance and what steps are made to follow. I will be going by Day at a time articles of Commands given… for an appropriate length for the book. I just want to give the reader an idea of what is done to attribute the Service Dogs to Commands, but I want to leave them room and capability to read over the Canine Support Teams Assistance Dog Program Training Manual on their own to get ready to take the class themselves for a Service Dog of their own!

Now, onto the Commands!

It started out with the verbal command of "Follow" with a solid tone and a happy voice. At the same time, I waved my right hand from behind my rear to the end of my rear, moving it forwards. And at that I began to walk out the door to my room. She listened and she followed me, but immediately moved forwards of me instead of behind like she was supposed to be and saw Krishna coming out of the kitchen and immediately ran up to her. That wasn't appropriate. Then I walked back to my room and she followed me like she remembered the command!

I gave her one treat for it, as a reward.

I stood up and waved my right hand towards my butt and said to Paige the Command of "Let's Go". I started to walk to the kitchen, and she followed me up close. We arrived down the hallway and I gave her a treat. She stood up like she was waiting for more Commands. So, I began to walk towards the bathroom and waved my hand towards my butt and said "Follow" again. This time she stopped halfway to the bathroom and when I arrived there, I noticed it, so I told her to "Follow!" again. She did immediately and came all the way to the bathroom and watched me pee. I then gave her a treat and told her "Good Job!" as a reward. She liked it!

Then I lay down on my bed in my room and she stood next to me, waiting for another command. I sat up and told her to "Come Here", and to that she walked up right next to me. Then I took my right hand and patted my face so that she would know that my next command of "Kiss" was telling her to lick my face. She didn't. She put her paw up like she wanted to shake my hand. I said "Kiss" again and put my head down where she could reach it. She batted her nose forwards to my hand and batted my hand with her nose! That was her method of giving a Kiss!

I gave her a treat for that one.

In response to her trying to shake my hand, I put out my hand to her and said: "Shake Hands!" with a smile and a cheery sound. She put her paw up and shook my hand. She does that when she wants a treat. So, I gave her one. Then, to complete that first day's list of Commands I told her to "Settle Down" because she kept on begging me for more treats and she had had enough of them. She calmed down and lay down. She was calm the rest of the night, too.

Paige likes the Commands! And she likes to do things for her handler! Good Dog!

I need to work on my Commands with her. I need to, before giving a Command, get it in my mind what I am going to do for it for a hand-and-arm signal at the same time as the Command. That would help a lot. It would help Paige to understand what it is that I am requesting her to do, too.

Now onto the second day's Commands.

In the Coffee Shop, I told Paige to get "Down" while waving my hand palms down from the upwards to the downwards position. She listened and lay down. I gave her a treat as a reward. Then I told her to "Roll Over", which was supposed to get her to roll over and put her belly in the air for a veterinarian to do their assessment. Instead Paige stood up and tried to shake my hand for a treat. When I gave the command, I had moved my hand with my forefinger up front in a circle to simulate the dog's body going in a circle. It didn't work. That was not listed as a hand and arm signal… none were in the books I had… so I had to make them up myself. Anyways, it didn't work.

So, I told Paige "Down" again with the hand signal and she got down and I gave her a treat. I am trying to bring her around to doing the Roll Over Command. Later I am going to have her get down and I am going to try to move her with my hand, so she knows to roll over.

As we were leaving the garage to go to the Coffee Shop I gave Paige the Command of "Go Through" in an attempt to get her to walk backwards in the thin space between the Van and the chair and scooter. She walked forwards at first, which was the wrong way, so I pulled on her leash to get her to go backwards and kept saying the command "Back" to her. She turned around and put her butt towards the door of the garage then gradually began to walk backwards towards it. She walked about three steps backwards, then turned around and started to walk to the front. So, she doesn't really get it, yet. No rewards.

I am going to work on the Commands of "Go Through" and "Back" every time we go through the garage until she gets it down… and probably some after that to reinforce the Command and what it means with her. I want her to think about getting a treat when she follows a command, so I want her to Think about what she is doing when I give her a Command.

Yesterday, when it was night and I was laying on my bed watching TV Paige came over to me and begged for treats. I pointed to her bed on the floor in my room and said to her: "Go to Bed". She immediately paused for a bit, then stopped begging for treats and went over to her bed and lay down on it, with her head UP because she still wanted me to come over and give her some treats. So, I walked over to the bed and took a handful of Pupperoni out of my bag for her and gave it to her to eat. She was so happy! Then she stayed there on the bed and went to sleep. What a good Dog! She is such an excellent pup; you would believe it if you saw her in action! Definitely! Perhaps me explaining her magnificent actions is enough for you to get her full appreciation! I hope so!

That concludes all the Commands for Day 2, except the Command of "Don't". That means that the handler wants the Service Dog to NEVER do the action that it is doing. At the VA Hospital, Paige started to bark at another dog that was there, and I told her: "Don't (bark)!" and she stopped but kept moving like she wanted to sic it. I don't know how to make the sic motion stop. There is no command in the book for that. So, I think that Paige hasn't been trained not to want to sic a bad dog. Oh well. She does fine, and her wanting to do things to protect me is definitely fine in my book. I appreciate it. It is a showing of kindness to me that Paige doesn't have to do but does on a regular basis. She is such a good Dog! I gave her a treat as a reward for not barking.

Now, onto Commands for Day 3.

I read over the commands for Day 3 yesterday and thought about them. There were two commands that I had never used on Paige at all, and the instructors of the course for her in 2017 didn't say anything about using them. They were the commands of "Speak", which is supposed to get the Dog to bark, and "Quiet", which is designed to get the Dog to stop barking. But I thought I would try them anyways.

At first, today, I took Paige for a walk with my rollator across the street from Krishna and Forest. As we were walking a lady came out with a tiny rottweiler, I think, and Paige started to bark at it with Forest. She was moving aggressively like she wanted to sic it! I told her loudly "Don't!" and tugged on her leash adding stress to her collar around her neck. She stopped barking and moving aggressively but kept on moving like she was trying to move towards the dog. Horrible! But she had obeyed the command of "Don't", and that was good.

We made our way back to the house and went inside. Paige lay down on the floor and looked at me as I walked into my room. I turned around and went and stood in front of her about 8 feet away and told her the command "Heel!", which meant that she was to join my left side next to my leg and sit if I was stationary. She did just that, walking behind me and to my left side, and she put her paw up to shake my hands for a treat. I gave her some snacks, about three of them, and went in my room and thought about the other commands I was going to give her.

I forgot most of the commands for Day 3, so I am going to have to read over them again. I remember "Side", which is to bring the Dog to the right side to sit when stationary. I remember that there is the command of "Snuggle", which is to do something that I don't remember to bring the Dog into your company... either put their head on your lap or on your shoulder or somewhere. I don't remember! I am going to have to go over the commands again to give them to Paige.

Getting up to go to the garage from my room I gave Paige the Command to go to my "Side", which is to sit on my right side. She did it without sitting... she stood... but I gave her a treat anyways. She doesn't have the sitting part down well to the Heel and Stand Commands. I shall work on it with her. Although, I don't know how to encourage her to sit down... Perhaps some gentle pressure put on her butt to make her want to crouch down. That would work!

When we were going through the garage to go to get on the bus to the Coffee Shop, I sat in the chair with Paige next to me. We waited. After about 20 minutes the bus showed up and pulled next to our parking lot. I stood up and told Paige the Command of "Go Through" to get her to start to walk backwards through the space between the van and my scooter. She didn't walk backwards. So, no reward and no treat. She was probably confused because I had walked in there with her straight to sit on the chair... so she was expecting that to be Forwards. The next command after "Go Through" is the command of "Back", which instructs the Dog to walk backwards. Oh well. She didn't do it, so I am going to have to work on those two Commands.

I have been using the Command of "Come Here" to get Paige to come to me to get her dressed, when the Command in the book is actually just "Come". And the Dog is supposed to sit down, which Paige doesn't do. I am worried that my error in Commands is going to cause me to fail the test that I have once per year. I have about five to six months before my next test, I think, so that should be time to go over the Commands with Paige and get the actions somewhat corrected. That will take some thinking on my part.

Now, more about the Commands of Day 3! Some of these Commands I have never used with Paige. Commands like "Say Hello", "Feet", or "Snuggle" have not been used on her by me. But she is a member of PAWS for Wounded Veterans, which is a Service Dog Program that probably taught her all the Commands on the list given to us by the Canine Support Teams when they had her… which for me was about 3 years ago! So, her memory may have faded on certain commands… I am sure it has because of the ways she doesn't do all the Commands that I know I have given her in the past. But I will work on it while I can! And definitely while I am writing this book!

I gave her the command of "Come Here" to get her to come over to me today so that I can get her dressed to go to the Coffee Shop. She did it readily, then got a snack, then lay down on her bed and rested until we left. She is still there. We will be leaving soon. I am waiting to give her more commands or questions about Science until the house is calmer. Granted, Krishna is asleep after work right now, but I just am not in the mood. That explains that! I will be more in the mood later.

A hesitation in the Commands for Paige to talk about something else for a minute. I am going to start to give her the command of "Sit" or "Down" when she begs me for a treat. Canine Support Teams, Inc. trainers told me during the course that we were not to give the Dogs treats unless they did something special. So, I am going to give her a Command to follow in order to earn a treat before I give her one.

Yesterday was the first time of trying it out. I saw her coming up and putting her paw up to give me a handshake. Instead of shaking her hand, I told her to "Sit". At first, she just stood there, so I waited a few seconds for her to process the Command. Then I told her to "Sit" again. The second time she did sit down. A second later she raised her paw up while she was sitting to give me a handshake and to continue to beg me for some treats. So, this time, because she was sitting down when she did it, I shook her hand. Then I gave her a couple of little treats. She gobbled them up while she was sitting down. That was delightfully good of her to do!

Then she stood up and walked around, and I let her. She walked for about a minute or so. Then, while I was sitting on my bed, she came over to me and sat down right in front of me. Then, she put her paw up to beg for another treat. That was evidence that she had learned that I wanted her to sit down to get a treat! I shook her hand and as she sat down gave her a treat to enjoy. And enjoy it she did!

I went to the Coffee Shop to write today, and Paige sat down immediately and put her paw up to my hand to beg for a treat. See… she learns quickly! I shook her paw and gave her a treat. She was so happy! She begged me for another because she was hungry, so I shook her paw and gave her another one. She smiled at me as she ate it. Then she finished and lay down on the ground in the "Down" position. She rests like that. While she was in the Down position, she raised her paw up and held it up. She wanted me to shake her paw again. So, I did, and I gave her a third treat. It was an hour before her eating time, so it was understood that she was hungry at that time. That was why she was eating so many treats. I wasn't going to get picked up for another 40 minutes, and I was running out of treats. So, I put the remainder away... a couple of them... and Paige lay down and put her head on the ground like she was going to sleep. She does that when she wants to rest and just look around. Her eyes were still open. That is how I could tell she was still awake.

Now, onto the remainder of Day 3 Commands.

I used the Command of "Out" to get Paige to leave the inside of the Coffee Shop and depart to the outside. She did it readily, but she usually follows that sort of movement without commands, so I don't know if it was really due to her following my order.

Earlier I was sitting in a chair next to a table against two walls. I was at the edge of one wall and the table, with the other edge of the table away from me against the long wall. I pulled on Paige's leash and told her to "Stand". She did. Then I pointed my finger at the space under the table between the table and the floor and said the Command "Go In". Paige looked at it hard and could see that if she lay down there, she would be over the stand for the table that ran along the floor. That would be uncomfortable for her and she knew it, so she didn't go get "Down" under the table. The "Go In" command is supposed to drive your Service Dog to go lay down under a table with their paws tucked in out of the walkway. But if there is something that makes it uncomfortable for the Dog, they won't do it. I learned that the hard way.

I used the rest of my time there to go over the rest of the commands, per day, that I had left in the book on Canine Support Teams Service Dog Class. I looked and saw that there were commands up to around day #5. I was on day #3 as I wrote this. I will need items to give to Paige to hold in her jaw when I do day #4. So, I am going to have to look around my room and into the desk and the drawer in my desk for objects to give to Paige to Command her to pick it up in her jaw and hold it, then give it back to me. There is more to it than just that, but the book is put away right now and I will get to that part when I start to do it tomorrow.

Today is the 7th of January. Me and Krishna took Paige to the mall. We took her to the store whose name I am not putting in here for privacy, but that we students of the Canine Support Teams go to once per year with our Service Dog for the test of Commands.

We went in there and Krishna had me take a basket with me and leave her my cane. I walked to an open area on the other side of the store. Then I gave Paige the Command of "Sit". She didn't sit down. So I told her again. And again, she didn't do it. So, I pulled a treat out of my treat pouch and held it in the same hand I was giving her the upwards-hand motion to Sit. And she listened and considered the treat, and she sat down. So, good of her to do it!

Then I gave her the Command of "Stay". She stayed sitting down and I took off with the cart through the store. Then I came back after about 30 seconds and Paige was still stilling in the same place. She hadn't followed me or anything. So good of her to do! When I returned to her I put my hand in my treat pouch and got one for her. I gave her the treat and she really enjoyed it, staying sat down in the same place for it.

Krishna told me to go ahead and do it all again. First, I had to go back to the entrance to the store and to go back in with Paige. I led her by her leash. We once again got to an open spot in the store and I gave her a treat. Then I told her to Stay and took off walking. Once again, she remained in position and allowed me to walk even in a different location. I returned to her and gave her a treat. She ate it wholeheartedly, feeling properly as though she deserved the treat.

After that, Krishna told Paige that she had done a really good job. Then Krishna congratulated me for doing such a find job of going through the Commands with Paige. She asked me if I would accept her buying me a hotdog on the way out of the mall. I agreed and got one. I ate it at the house. It was delicious!

That was it for Commands for that period of time. I shall continue with more later. The next edition will be about how I talked Paige into getting and holding objects in her jaws, bring them to me, then give them over. There are a lot of Commands in that edition.

Today I experimented with Paige by laying out a Kong ball and telling her the Command of "Look", followed by the Command "Get it". Paige refused to listen. She just sat there, looking at the Kong. She had sat up from laying down as soon as I told her to get it. She had the orders deep in her mind and what she was supposed to do... but in her forefront mind there was hesitation. Granted, there were a lot of Commands involved!

But she had looked intently at the Kong when I Commanded her to "Look". But when I motioned towards it with my hand and said the Command "Get it" ...which was supposed to make her pick it up in her jaw...Paige ignored the Command and just kept staring at the Kong. I eventually concluded that Paige didn't want to follow that series of Commands. So, I changed them.

She was standing up. I didn't want that, so I reached into my treat pouch and grabbed her two little pieces of Pup-Peroni. I held them in front of her mouth and raised my hand upwards, saying "Sit". She sat and looked at my hand with treats. She wanted them. I held onto them and told her the Command of "Down ". She lay down and I have her the two treats. She rested her head down.

Then I held my hand up and stationary and told her firmly "Stay". Then I turned my back to her and began to walk away. I walked out of sight of her and around the van. Then, when I walked back around the van and looked at her, I could see that she had listened to the Command and was laying in the same spot! What a darn fine Dog! I walked over to her and gave her another treat as a reward!

For the next two days we went to the cabin up in Green Valley Lake. I lay down and listened to the radio on my headphones on the bed in the front room. It was a Queen-sized bed, so it was big enough to give Paige the Command of "Up!" while patting my right hand on the top of the cushion of the bed. Paige heard it and immediately jumped up and lay down on top of the bed. Her head was out in a protective fashion for me. She was very relaxed and attentive.

After we spent two days up at the cabin, we came down the windy hill on the curvy roads with Paige going through the motions in the back of the SUV that we took them in. She was resting with Forest, the non-Service dog. He was crying a lot. It took us an hour and a half to get back to the house. We passed the road going to Paige's yearly test, on the way home. We got there down the windy roads and eventually the freeway and took all the gear inside. I left Paige dressed in her vest and collar so she could be ready to take the test. Then, ready, we put Paige into the backseat of the car and me and Krishna got in and we went to the store where we were going to have the test. It was a shopping mall store of sorts. I am not going to put the name of it down for protection of their privacy. It is a nice store, though, I am sure of that!

We parked the car and Krishna and I and Paige got out and went walking over to the front of the store looking for an Instructor from the Canine Support Teams to meet up with us. There was a lady that we knew there. She is a delightful woman, young, and really intelligent. I have worked with her before. If I remember right... and it was a long time ago... she was one of the instructors of the class I took to become Paige's handler. The lady recognized us and said "Hi!" She also said hi to Paige. Then she explained the questions and training she was going to have me do.

We went inside the store and in the front was a long walkway next to some aisles that went next to counters with products on it. The lady, I don't remember her name, said that I was to take Paige over to an open area and tell her to "Sit", then "Down", then "Stay". I figured that would be easy, and I had treats to give to Paige. So, I took out a treat and held it in front of her and told her to "Sit" while giving her the sit hand and arm signal. But Paige refused to listen. There were other people walking in the store and she was distracted. So, I told her again. Then again. And again. And she kept on standing up! Finally, she looked at my hand and sat down. Then I told her to get "Down". Again, she hesitated and spent her time sitting down and looking elsewhere. So I told her in a very kindly tone of voice "Down" ... and she got down partway. So, I told her "all the way Down..." and she lay all the way down.

At that the instructor was standing next to me and she said that I needed to stop being so resilient with my commands and be more kind and nicer and upfront with how I say to Paige to do certain things. "There is something wrong with her. She is not wanting to listen to your commands. That is different than the way she listened to you when you were in the Class. Try to do it this way..." And with that she raised her voice up and made it sound really friendly and she said to Paige while moving her hands: "Sit!" Paige sat down immediately. Then the lady told me to give her a treat. So, I gave her a piece of Pup-Peroni. Then the lady said "Down" and moved her hand in a downwards manner, standing tall when she did it and using the kindly voice. Paige immediately lay down all the way. I gave her another treat for that action. Then the lady told me that I needed to give Paige the Commands like she is, even though I can't raise my voice as high as she is because I am a male and she is a female. I agreed with her.

"Let's go into the cafeteria and talk about it. There is something wrong with her that she is not listening to the Commands you are giving her." The lady went and sat down in the cafeteria. I went and sat down next to her.

Krishna sat at a table next to us and listened, giving her input from time to time.

"I think that Paige got worn out from the trip we just took her on. She had to ride in the back of the SUV with a dog that isn't a Service Dog for about an hour and a half down from the mountains that we had her at for the previous two days. I didn't really do any tricks with her there. The road was really windy going down from up there. She was probably weaving and bobbing around on the way down. That was probably in her mind, being stuck in the back of an SUV with a whining non-Service dog. That probably distracted her." I tried to explain it in detail. The lady listening was really smart, so she was able to ascertain the full details of what had probably happened.

"That makes sense. I can how a Dog's personality can draw into it conclusions that are not in lieu of the environment around it. Dog's can draw conclusions about things that are really intelligent, especially a Dog that is a really smart Golden Doodle like yours. There is another reason that you haven't noticed, either, I think."

"What is that?"

"Your Dog is getting fat. She is putting on too much weight. If she doesn't slim down, she is going to wind up getting separated from being a Service Dog. They are meant to be thin, because thin Dogs do the tricks and follow Commands and don't eat too much food and snacks. What kind of snacks are you giving her? They looked big."

I pulled a Pup-Peroni treat out of my bag. They were all the same size. It was about ½ inch by ¼ inch in size. I gave it to her.

"That is way too big. You said you were giving her two of those per snack? And you are giving her two full cups of food per day to eat? One cup per meal for two meals… right?"

"That's right. Is that making her fat?"

"You need to reduce the amount of treats you give to her by ¼ the size of what you are giving her. Those Pup-Peroni have sugar in them. And as far as food goes, until she loses weight, reduce the amount you give her to ½ cup per serving… for about a month. That will make her lose weight without starving her."

"Oh. Ok. I can do that. So, I failed the test. We need to get her certification because I am going with Krishna on a vacation on an airplane and they need the card for Paige. Can I still get one, even though we failed the test?"

"You will get a temporary one. I'll call you when we are done. Now, for the rest of the test we are just going to walk around the area and give me an opportunity to see how you react to Paige. I know she is having a bad day right now. So, I will take that into consideration."

And with that, we began to walk around the square around the middle of the store, down aisle after aisle.

Mox walked right next to me and looked at me walking Paige. I talked to her about how I paid attention to Paige and how she performed at things.

Then, as we were walking, Paige began to sniff at the products on the counters. Mox told me that she wasn't supposed to do that, and that I should pull on her leash to get her to stop, then release it as a reward when she stops. So, I saw Paige begin to sniff at another box of goodies on the counter, and I pulled very lightly on her leash. It didn't stop her. I was used to pulling very lightly on the leash when she was being counselled because I didn't want to hurt her. But it turns out that I wasn't pulling hard enough to get my message across. Mox (the lady's name that was the Instructor of the test was named Mox) told me to give her the leash so she could show me what was supposed to be done.

I gave Mox the leash and she walked with Paige until she saw her sniff at the leg of another customer. Mox pulled firmly on the leash and tightened the leash on the collar around Paige's next by pulling upwards and forwards on it. Then she immediately released it. Paige was okay during the event, but she felt it. She didn't sniff at anyone again after that, for about 15 minutes. That was so good of her! Mox told me that what I was doing was wrong. I was pulling way too gently on the leash and it wasn't teaching Paige a lesson. And the way I was pulling it… forwards… was making it so that Paige would react by walking more forwards and that could make me fall down. "Pull up and to the side with the leash, and that will make her want to walk to the side. That will make it so you don't fall down. But you pull too gently on it anyways. You need to pull harder to send the message to her!" That was a good lesson. Mox used really large words because she was really intelligent. And pleasant.

I took the leash and watched for Paige to sniff at anything she wasn't supposed to sniff at. She didn't. Mox said that she was going to hesitate from doing it again because she had just learned a lesson from it and because she was an intelligent Golden Doodle she would keep the lesson in memory as she moved forwards. So, I didn't pull on the collar for about 15 minutes as I walked with her. Then, she moved suddenly to sniff at the leg of a customer. I immediately pulled very firmly on her leash in a sideways direction and she immediately stopped. I didn't have to tell her to stop it or anything. That was good. The lesson was working. And I remember it. For example, I am writing this part of this document the next day after the test, and I remember the details of what had occurred. That means that I will remember it for a while!

We finished walking around the store and got to the beginning by the doors again. Mox told me that I could go before the Canine Support Teams for an event that would be a refresher of the Commands and the raising of the Dog so that I could take the test right after and pass it. Mox had a handout paper form that had the test score indicator that she was supposed to fill out that was still blank. She said that I had failed the test, for now, but that she was going to give me a temporary acceptance letter for me and Krishna to use for our trip next week on the plane that we needed to get Paige allowed on the plane by showing it to the staff of the airline. So, that will be okay. I am going to take the test right before we go. Next week sometime, I think.

I thanked Mox and told her that she was doing a remarkable job. I told her that we would not take Paige up to the Cabin before the test again so that she would be able to pass with flying colors. I had told Mox that Paige had followed the commands just a few days before we had gone there at the store in my hometown and she did so readily. But we did it in a different part of the store. There were not as many people walking around. So, she wasn't distracted. We'll fix that before the next time I come for the test. Mox thanked me and said that I did a good job. "Just make sure you pull on the leash firmly and to the side. And you will get her to stop sniffing!" That was so nice of Mox. And with that we departed company, and Krishna and Paige and I went back to the car and got in and went home.

The next day Paige had had time to sit around the home and to go outside with no issues. She rested and she pooped outside. We picked it up, like usual. Then, the next day, I woke up and went to the counter in the kitchen and there I cut the Pup-peronis that I had in the bag into 4 pieces per item. I put them back in the bag. Then I went back to my room and I pulled out one of the tiny Pup-peronis. I told Paige to "Sit" and moved my hand upwards with the treat in sight in it. She sat down and looked at the treat. I gave it to her. Then I pulled out another treat, and told her "Down", while I said that I was moving my hand in a downwards manner towards her. She lay down. I gave her a treat as a reward. Then I told her to "Stay". I gave her another treat. She stayed put, even after she had eaten the treat.

So that was proof that she was ready to do the Commands. She had just been interrupted by the trip down from the mountains in the back of the SUV for an hour and a half. At least I know that she is ready to do the Commands. I am certain that I will pass the test next time. Granted, I am going to have to get in the habit of pulling on her leash when she starts to sniff things. I have to carry the leash around the short handle to do it, too, and that I am not used to doing with her. But I am working on it. She has to get used to me walking with her holding onto the short handle. That takes a certain degree of readiness on my grip on my part as the handler. So, we are both going to work on it. I am in the Coffee Shop right now, and I have been walking with Paige and my Rollator, holding onto her on the short handle. She has been trying to walk really slow, because she wants to walk away from the wheels of the Rollator. But it is hard to hold onto her short handle and have her keep distance away from it without losing my grip. I don't know what to do to prevent her losing step or walking in an interrupted fashion while holding onto the short leash and walking with the Rollator at the same time.

Perhaps I just need to adjust her collar around her

neck so that it releases the leash along the top of the neck, rather than flowing the leash down to the lower side where the head gets in the way. There is more room to move with it there, anyways. Perhaps that is what I will start to do. It will only take a little bit of getting use to, moving that collar around when she is stationary.

(Now write about tugging on and releasing the leash to stop her from smelling people or sniffing products. A form of counselling and reward.)

ANOTHER PERIOD OF TIME WITH PAIGE

I was sitting on Krishna's bed watching TV today and it was Paige's dinner time. Paige came up to me and rubbed her head really roughly on my fingers of my hand like she wanted me to pet her snout. So, I started to pet her shout and she moved her head to the side so I couldn't anymore. So, I rested my hand still... and what did she do? She moved her head next to my hand AGAIN with a sense of urgency. The idea I got was that she wanted to be pet. So, I tried to pet her again. Again, she moved her head off to the side. Then it occurred to me...

Darn, the Dog wants some food!

So, I said "Let's Go!" to her and began to walk to the pantry where we keep the bucket of food. I took the ladle out of the container and picked a cup of food and put it in her dish for eating. Then I walked with it and Paige following me to my room. I put the dish on the floor in there and said "Dinnertime!" and left it at that. I shut the TV off so no commercials with dogs in them would interrupt Paige from eating.

And at that Paige began to eat her food. She was hungry, and she liked it a lot!

After a spell she had finished her food and went into the hallway to sit in her spot there. Then she lay down and acted like she went to sleep. She does that a lot… acts like she is asleep when she is really awake. That is her body position during most of the day. It makes it a little more difficult for me to give her many commands, though. I can't really give her a command that she will listen to if she is laying down and resting her head on the floor. But I try, and sometimes it works out okay. Depends on what state her personality is during that day or night. Sometimes she *wants* me to give her Commands. Other times she doesn't. It depends on her mood.

Krishna came home today at 9am, the usual time she gets off work. She came into the house and was saying all kinds of kind things to Paige, petting both Paige and Forest, and rubbing her bump on her butt. Paige liked it and waggled her head back and forth in excitement. And Krishna was singing to her! I don't remember the lyrics… this happened about 5 hours ago… but it was a happy song. Krishna played with the dogs for about 15 minutes. I wanted to walk them the whole time.

Eventually, I got tired of just sitting there with her playing with the dogs and not walking them, so I said to her: "Come on. Let's take the Dogs for a walk now."

She interrupted me by saying that she didn't want to take the Dogs for a walk. She wanted to: "take a nap". She said that she was tired. I immediately got upset. I thought it was extremely stupid to play with the Dogs for 15 minutes when one is too tired to take them for a walk. I told her that she was stupid and left in a rage. I went outside with the dogs and listened to my headphones from my iPhone.

I sat out there for about 10 minutes and Krishna came out and asked me if I wanted some coffee that she would make for me. "GO TO SLEEP!" I yelled at her! I was sick and tired of her dragging her feet with other things when she could have been walking the dogs... but was wasting her time doing other things that were unrelated to it!

She got all upset and yelled at me. Said I was "wasting my time" when SHE was guilty of it! She went back inside. I thought that she was just finally going to go to sleep.

So, did she?

NO, SHE DIDN'T.

Instead she ignored me and went into the house and made some coffee in a cup and brought it out to me. I told her that she was being remarkably stupid and that she needed to go to sleep. "You have been running around playing with the dogs and doing other things besides walking the dogs for the last 30 minutes! That's twice as long as it takes to talk the dogs! What is your damned problem?"

"Shut up you hypocrite! You aren't walking the dogs!" she stymied.

"I'm sitting on the couch outside with them because you won't walk them with me, you bitch!" I countered.

"I have been busy getting the dogs water and feeding Sunshiney and feeding Forest food, man! I have been busy!" she was really uptight and didn't realize that she didn't need to do any of those things because all that she had to do was ask me to do it… and I would have!

I told her that she was an idiot and that was unnecessary because I would have done it if she asked me. She got all upset and left, yelling at me. Then she went to sleep, about 35 minutes after she came home. Stupid idiot. She should have walked the Dogs with me. What a fool to think that they would be satisfied with her ignoring them or foolhardily petting them and then refusing to walk them because she was suddenly "too tired". She is a stupid bitch sometimes.

That happened some 5 hours ago, and I am still pissed off at her idiocy. And Paige is not happy, either.

Paige was inside of Krishna's room today, and I was laying on Krishna's bed watching my computer. The cat was on the bed watching TV. Paige came running over and barked at Sunshiney. A lot! Krishna was sitting next to her and told her "Go! Go! Leave her alone!" Paige ran out of the room and then ran back in, barking at Sunshiney some more. Krishna told her again to Go and she left then.

"Why does that damn dog go after Sunshiney that-a-ways?" She was upset with Paige. "That horrible dog is an archive of mistrust and anguish!"

"She's a Dog, Krishna. That is why she does it. She is just being a Dog. She didn't bite her or anything. She just barked. She can do that, can't she?" I was trying to defend Paige from Krishna's negative statements.

Then there was a dog shown on the TV and Paige began to bark at it, too. Krishna yelled at her to stop. "Paige, you've been digging in the dirt outside and you have mud on your face and you smell like ass!" said Krishna firmly to Paige. Paige liked the attention and put her face onto Krishna's lap and got a kiss from her. "Now go on Paige, go on! I can't pet you all day long!" And with that Paige walked down the hallway.

That was another rough time with Paige. See, she was a Service Dog that had excellent character, but there were times when she would act out and do things that were not positive. I didn't like it, but I tried to do my best to react to her positively. It was in her character to obey orders and commands and to do the things that we guided her to do. So, there was no issue with that, either. The only thing she really did that had no control involved was to bark at other dogs and move like she wanted to sic them. Then I had to pull on the leash to get her to stop and I would give her the command of "Quiet" but she never listened and kept on trying to get the other dog. Good thing that the leash is strong, and she can't break free of it.

Later on, this afternoon, I was laying on Krishna's bed and she brought Sunshiney out of my room and into her bedroom and put her on the same bed that I was laying on. As she did, she sat down and began to pray. Paige came running over and crouched up with her front legs on the bed and started to bark at Sunshiney. I told her: "Don't! Stop it!" She didn't listen. Krishna told her to stop and leave the room. She ignored her. Then she moved to the other side and stood on her hind legs and put her front legs up on the bed and started to bark at Sunshiney again! Horrible! Sunshiney got all upset and jumped off of the other side of the bed away from Paige and ran underneath it to get away from Paige. Then Krishna kept on praying and Paige ran out of the room defeated and went to the living room.

Man, Paige went outside in the back yard today and we found her with a lizard in her mouth! She was holding it in her teeth and didn't let us in to get it out! And we commanded her to release it over and over again and she refused to listen. She even started, when we gave the commands to let it go, to walk away from us with it to keep it away from us! Then she would stand there with it in her teeth. Then she would release it on the ground, waggle her head around it, then pick Then it up again.

Eventually, she dropped it down when I was standing there, and I immediately picked it up and threw the dead body of the lizard into the trash can. she listened to our command of "Let's Go!" and followed me into the house with her jaw clean of the lizard.

Paige sometimes gets it in her head to do the thing that she wants to do with no consideration for what other people want to do. And her picking up a lizard was a selfish-principled thing. She obviously didn't care about the well-being of the lizard. If she did, she wouldn't have picked it up and killed it with her jaw in the first place. And she held onto it instead of listening to our commands. That was willful ignorance of them. That was inappropriate. I don't know what to do with her to get her to stop doing such things. Gladly, she very rarely does it. So, at least there is THAT going for her!

My television in my room is broken. It doesn't get a screen on and the screen that it has is white and black spots buzzing throughout. Then it shuts down. I think the TV is broken. So, I am going to Krishna's brother's room that he comes and visits us in sometimes, separated by months in between, and I watch the TV in there.

When I watch the TV in the other room, Paige comes in there to protect me and she lays down on the floor of the room with her head down but her eyes open. She can hear down there too; I know this because when a dog comes in on the commercials and starts to bark, she waggles her ears around and raises her head. So, she is showing me that she can hear the dogs barking. That is good of her. I am glad that she has that sense about her.

It is a good thing that she comes in and protects me throughout the meeting with me. She is always protecting me. She likes me to be comfortable. So, I try to avoid confrontations with other people. I don't have those anyways, because of my mellow nature… but I do it even less with Paige in my company. She is such a great Dog! Usually to protect me she likes to stay calm and keep her eyes open. To stay really calm she lays down and looks out at people. Mostly she listens. She can hear the movement of people at tables or walking through a room or such a thing. That is how she keeps her attention open to doing things that are ready and able to be protective of me, her handler. She likes me. She likes me to be comfortable. And she likes me to be safe.

Me and Krishna are driving with Paige in the SUV to the Antique Store in another city to purchase a couple of tables for Krishna for Christmas. That will be nice. Paige will be riding in the trunk of the SUV with the door down. There is room for her back there to lay down and ride along. There are three windows around it that she can look out of, if she wants to. She usually doesn't, though. She just lays down and enjoys the trip. Krishna drives at a very safe speed and she doesn't jerk the vehicle around with the steering wheel, so there is no drama to the rides. She is a great driver. And Paige likes it. Sometimes she looks up over the holder between the seats at us in the front and says "Hi". That shows that she is such a great Dog, you can imagine!

Paige isn't always a good Dog, though. Yesterday, our other dog Forest was eating some food in Krishna's room and Paige wanted to bolt in there and eat some of it. Forest started to growl at her, and Paige ignored him and jumped over the dish and started to eat. Forest growled at her a lot, and Paige got all upset and jumped on him! She pinned him to his back and started to growl really loudly at him, barking and everything! She didn't bite him, but she was waggling her jaws near his face like she was threatening him with a bite if he kept growling at her. And growl is what he did!

I jumped over on top of Paige and tried to push her off. She had no collar or leash on... so I had nothing to grab ahold of. And she kept resisting. She had it in her head that she wanted to stand on top of Forest and growl. I eventually pushed her off and pushed her against the bed. She lay down and bent her head around trying to get past me. Eventually, I told her to "Go Now!" and walked her quickly over to my room! She followed me.

Once in my room, I put her collar with her leash on her and held on to her in the room while she calmed down. I kept her in there while I sat on my bed and she sat on the floor next to me on the leash for about an hour. Then I went with her into the kitchen and ate some olives in a jar. Then I let her go, and she didn't bite Forest or nip at him or do anything negative. That was good of her. I guess that the only thing she wanted was the food. Good thing it was gone by the time I let her go so she wouldn't get it in her head to go after Forest again.

Aside from that one incident, Paige acts like a really good Dog. The only other thing she does that I don't like is to get angry at other dogs that aren't Service Dogs, or at cats. She doesn't really like either one of the two. Now, there are some dogs that are not Service Dogs that she gets along with and is friendly with. But there are others that I think she can tell that they would bite their owners or someone else that she barks at and moves like she wants to sic them. That is troubling, because I have to keep control of her on her leash when she does such a thing… and I am worried that the leash will break and that she will go out jumping after the dog and bite them. That would be no good. It would alarm and anger the dog's owner and maybe lead to a confrontation. I don't want someone telling me that I need to put my Dog down. That would be no good.

Today is December 17th, 2019 and Krishna and I are going with Paige in the car to the kennel of Canine Support Teams in another town. It is down the street when Paige was born. We are going there to give them presents for Christmas! They are such fine people, and they deserve the best!

We made two presents and filled out two cards for them. One is a box of cookies and a Christmas card for Canine Support Teams. I called a lady that works there on the phone today and found out what time they are going to be there, because Krishna had to sleep today since she worked last night, and she wouldn't be able to drive there tired without getting in a wreck without sleeping first. They said that they would be there until about an hour and a half after she wakes up, so we will be able to make it on time! Nice! I also asked her if Carol Roquemore, who is the owner of Canine Support Teams, Inc., is going to be there so we could give her a present. She said that she was leaving early because she was handicapped, but the staff could give her the present later tonight when they go to her house to sing her Christmas carols. I said that was okay and asked how long they were going to be singing carols. They told me half an hour and asked if I wanted to go to it. I said: "Yes! We would!" Then I got off the phone.

The lady sent me a message on my phone that said that she had made a mistake. The staff was going to be singing carols tomorrow... not tonight like she said. I wrote her back and said that was okay. We were not going to be able to make it tomorrow. But we would be up there tonight to drop off the presents. She responded with a: "Thank you!"

Carol is in a wheelchair and used to have Polio, so we got for her for Christmas an excellent blanket that she can wear on her lap and keep warm in the cold weather. It is stamped with levels of red and green and grey stripes on it and it looks really nice. I also made her a Christmas card that says a lot of nice things about Paige on it and thanks her for giving me such an Excellent Service Dog! She was such a great instructor during the course that I went to in order to get Paige. She was there almost every day. She was available for us to ask questions to about our Dogs. We had our Dogs with us at the time of the course. I remember that at the very beginning - the first day – I didn't have Paige at the time, and Carol did an interview of me and asked me what kind of job I had. I was unemployed because I was handicapped, but I was an author who wrote books, so I told her that I was an unemployed author who would be published one day. She said: "Ok!" And she listened to me being an author and gave me a Dog with the name the describes what authors do… write Pages for books… a Dog named Paige! And she blended in nicely! I received Paige and got along with her famously! She is such a Great Dog!

So, Mrs. Roquemore did a really good job. All the instructors were great people. They really cared about the students. And they appreciated the military. They had a lot of military students or veterans there.

I hope they like their presents! They deserve them! I would write down if they enjoyed their presents in the next paragraph.

I am at the Coffee Shop with Paige and we are sitting inside and there is another non-Service Dog with its owners sitting outside under the canopy and visible through the window. Paige doesn't like it and she barked at it… and it barked back at her and paced around. Then I stopped her with a pull on her collar and a Command to "Leave It!" She did. Then I stood up with her and went to go get another drink.

I got a Rainbow Unicorn drink. No sugar in it. It is good for you.

As I got the drink, a lady came into the Coffee Shop with a little Golden Retriever that was 4 months old. He was hesitant and was wary. Paige really liked him and went up to him to sniff him a lot. He was wary of her. The lady with him told me his young age and that he was being trained to be a Service Dog. She got him for part of the time and the rest of the time went to his trainers. She liked that I was a good handler of my Service Dog. I told her about the grant that I had applied to 4 ½ years ago through the Canine Support Teams. I told her that they used the grant request to give birth to my Service Dog and to raise her for 2 years to be a Service Dog. Then they put me through a 2-week course to learn how to become her handler. She said that was divine! She liked to be her Golden Retrievers handler. It was an excellent Dog. It will make for a nice Service Dog.

The lady left with her Dog and I sat down and drank my Rainbow Unicorn drink. I finished it, and it became time for my ride to arrive in 10 minutes. That other dog is still sitting outside, so I am probably going to run into troubles with Paige when I depart. I am going to walk with her away from him on my walker so that I can pull on her leash if she acts out. Sometimes she is reckless around other dogs she doesn't like.

Ok, time for me to put my computer away and wait for my ride.

I did that and as I did Krishna came into the Coffee Shop and told me that she had forgotten her phone at home. I said ok and took the Rollator and Paige over to the counter to tell the staff that I was leaving. They said "Goodbye". I looked outside and sure enough the owners of the non-Service Dog outside could see that we were leaving, and they could tell that Paige and their dog were barking at each other and there would probably be an altercation if they passed each other. So, they took their dog to the back of the building in-place out-of-sight of the walkway to the exit. That was good. At that, Paige and I and Krishna went outside with no hazards and we made it to the car without any drama. We got in and drove home. I told Krishna about how Paige had been taught to do a trick for a treat…and she was intelligent because she learned quickly. Krishna liked the story and said yes to it.

Today is Christmas Eve, and we exchanged presents. Krishna invited both of her brothers over for the holiday.

They brought presents for me and Krishna and each other. Nice presents. And they brought a present for Paige and Forest. Initially, Paige got for Christmas a bag of Pupperoni – two of them – and they were sitting in the pantry. Then, when we were opening presents, Krishna's brothers brought over a see-through sock with doggy treats inside of it. Krishna opened it up and gave Paige a rawhide stick to chew on. She started to gobble it up!

Then we opened more presents. Krishna gave Forest a stick of rawhide to chew on. Then we finished opening the presents and me and Krishna played a game of checkers with the new checkers kit that I got as a gift.

She won! I played hard… but dropped the ball at the end of it and lost my pieces. She then ate me up.

Krishna and her two brothers and I went out to get something to eat at a steak house. We left Paige back at the rear because the steak house was going to be filled during Christmas Eve. It was a good choice. The place was rambled full of people. We had a really good meal there. Then we went back to the house. I hadn't fed Paige during that time, so she had a late dinner because I didn't want her to get full while we were gone and have to go to the bathroom when we were at the steakhouse and not at the house to let her go to the bathroom in the back yard. I didn't want her to poop in the house when we were gone. So, she was hungry when we returned.

The first thing she did when we got home was go into the kitchen. Then she came into my room while I was playing with Sunshiney. Paige had something in her mouth. I put my fingers together and put them into her mouth. She held her jaws closed until I pulled gently on her teeth, then she let the object go. It was the chewed-up rawhide slab that she had ben chewing on earlier! I gave it back to her, and she went back into the kitchen to eat it. Sunshiney came back on the bed and started to run her head on the edge of my leg in an effort to get me to pet her a lot. So, I pet her, and she liked it! She purred and purred at me!

Krishna told me after seeing Paige eating the rawhide that Dogs were not supposed to eat rawhide because it was hard for them to digest. It was a message from her trainers at Canine Support Teams. So, there was a solid message in that statement. So, we decided not to give the Dogs any more of the treats in the sock because they were bad for Dogs to eat. Instead we were just going to stick to giving her chicken treats of Pup-peronis or some other quality treat that we have to spend money on. Paige agreed. She didn't beg me for any more treats out of the sock. That was really good of her. And, so far, there has been no problems with her digestive system from eating the rawhide. I hope there is none that will happen.

That is all for Christmas Eve. It is 10:15 PM right now, so Paige is going to sleep. Good night!

On New Year's Eve I was laying in bed when midnight came around. Suddenly, fireworks started to go off in the neighborhood, making loud racketing noises. Paige immediately came into my room and put both of her paws on my bed, alarmed! She was worried from the noise that was going around! I began to pet her and tell her that it was okay. She was shuddering. Her rear legs were flexing back and forth with a worry that denied her presence... or rather put forth the presence of a worried Dog. She was moving her head side-to-side in an erroneous fashion, trying to see what was making the noise. But there was nothing but walls around her, so she couldn't see the source. Eventually, I got really concerned for her, and I told her the Command of "Up" to get her to get up on the bed. She did after a few spells.

She wouldn't lay down on the bed. There was too much noise form the fireworks. But she sat on the bed. Usually she would lay down up here and go to sleep... but not this time. She sat up and waved her head around looking up at the window shades, trying to look out at the fireworks.

Eventually, about 20 minutes later, the fireworks stopped. Paige calmed down and when it was silent outside, she lay down and put her head down after a spell. That was good of her to calm down. She was so stressed out that it worried me.

That was New Year's Eve/Day.

The next day Krishna got a painting from the Antique store of Yosemite National Park. It was large. It was about 6 feet in width and 5 feet in height. Big! Krishna tried to put it up over the couch in the front room on the wall with a couch underneath it but the screw in the wall to hold it up by the cord going from side to side along the top back of it was too low for the painting to ride over the top of the couch. When it was put on the painting rode down below the barrier between the couch and the wall. So, we left it unhooked and placed it over the couch against the wall and waited.

January 3rd came around, and Krishna summoned the neighbor who used to be in Army Special Forces to come and adjust the screw. He is a nice guy and came over to help with ease, or so it seemed at first. He screwed in a screw above the old one that was about 10 inches higher and put the painting into the screw with the help of Krishna holding up the other end of the painting. The neighbor put the cable around the back of the painting into the screw, and gently placed it down. The two of them left it up there and let go. It was holding against the wall, at first.

Then the right side of the cable came undone from the painting and the painting dropped down to the couch.

Krishna and the neighbor held the painting against the wall. The neighbor readjusted the cable to the side of the painting so it wouldn't come off it again. Then they both put the painting back up on the wall. It stayed steady there. Paige was standing on the floor next to the couch under the painting.

Me and Krishna and the neighbor started to walk out

the garage. As we did, I heard a smashing noise behind me. "Sounds like that painting just fell to the ground" I said. Krishna ignored me and kept on walking. I was worried, because what would happen if the painting fell on top of Paige? It was a big painting. Would it damage her? I didn't know.

Outside, we went to the neighbor's house to look at the crate-made doggie bed that he made for his dog. As we looked at it, I kept thinking that perhaps we should go back to the house to check on Paige. After a very short spell, I began to walk back to the house, and Krishna followed me.

When we went inside the house the painting had fallen across the couch and was laying sideways over the top of it. Paige was padding around with one leg raised up. She was shaking in her hind legs and her stomach and back. When we walked into the house by opening the door, she immediately came over to me and raised up her paw and was drooling. She looked horrible. It was clear that the painting had fallen on her and had applied pressure to her. I walked over to a chair next to the painting on the couch and sat down and immediately began to pet Paige, trying to analyze her for damage. She refused to move away from me, not like I tried to get her to move away, she just usually went on her own direction after a little while. She didn't this time. She stood there next to me, drooling, and waving her paw upwards to shake my hand for comfort over and over again. She didn't want a treat. I tried to give her a treat for shaking my hand, because that was her usual motive for it, but she wouldn't accept a treat from me. I started to think that her back was damaged from the weight of the painting.

Krishna got a chicken treat out of a bag of treats and gave it to Paige in the kitchen. Then, as she was eating it, Krishna and I went over to the painting and lifted it up on both ends and walked it over to the side room down the hallway. It was really hard to fit in there it was so big. But eventually we got it in there and stood it up on it's side.

Krishna departed the house to go get her neighbor during the incident to see if he could put the painting back on the wall. He said he would try to do it tomorrow. He said that he would probably be able to fix the other side of the cable that came undone. The cable had some issues with the way it was attached to the painting. First the one side came undone. Then we put it back on the wall and the other side came undone. As a matter of fact, I don't even want the painting to go back up on the wall. But Krishna wants it up there. Hopefully it doesn't break again.

"Take Paige into your room and close the door. We need to see what is wrong with her. That is a heavy painting." Krishna was really concerned about Paige. So, I agreed and walked into my room. Paige followed me really close to my right leg. She was worried that something else would fall on her and she felt that I was protective. I felt really bad that I had heard the painting fall and took some time to react to it. But we went into the room and I shut the door. Paige really wanted to stay close to me and wouldn't give me room to walk past her to my bed without me moving her with my leg. I sat down then, and she paced right next to me with her head near my lap.

I began to pet her a lot. She kept drooling and shaking and drooling some more. I was worried that there was something wrong with her back. But when I pet her, I ran my hands down her backside and saw all the way down her back was okay, so she probably didn't have any breaks or anything like that going on. But she was drooling a lot, and she would accept no treats.

I pet her nonstop with the door closed for half an hour. Then I started to think that we were going to have to take her to a veterinarian for a checkup. I opened the door and departed the room. Paige walked with me really close to my leg. I walked into Krishna's room and looked for her. She wasn't in there. I went all through the house looking for her. Then I looked in the parking area and her car was missing. She had gone somewhere else. So, frustrated, I went outside with Paige and Forest to the backyard and sat down on the couch out there.

Paige came up to me and begged for a treat. This time she took a couple of them. Then she walked down the concrete walkway to the other side and lay down. So, it was that she was actually okay. The painting had hurt her and she was worried about things falling on her, but her back was okay, her legs were actually okay (she could walk with rhythm), and her head and neck was okay, so the painting probably didn't cause much damage. Just distress. Thus the panting and drooling.

I am checking Paige over time for inflammation and other errors. Hopefully she is okay. I really like that Dog. She is a remarkable Service Dog and she didn't deserve to be a victim of bad construction of a painting. Even if it is a nice painting.

Paige has had a really troubling New Year. Hopefully it is not an indication of what the rest of her year is going to be like. It is, after all, 2020. Doubles and Mystery. That is what those numbers stand for. What is going to come of this year, I wonder?

Paige is an extremely helpful Dog. She helps me, with her presence and calmness, to write stories about things. It has only been three months so far, and I am ¾ of the way done with four different books. It is my hope that I will be done writing them by the time of three months from now, and that I will be able to get them edited and published afterwards. It is my hope that my current editor will edit more books than the one that he has edited so far. He is currently working on getting it published. We'll see how he does. He should get it published. I think that it is a divine book!

I have experience with writing nonfiction books that are resolute in imagination and thought. They seem like they are partly fictional, but they are based exclusively on reality. That is making me want to write more into the fictional world, but that takes full-on imagination. There is a difference between writing about things that you are actually doing versus writing about things that you are imagining are happening. It takes a different skillset to do so. So it takes some adaptation to do it. I am adapting. I am writing two fictional books right now that are ready in detail and form.

I have written two nonfiction books that have a lot said in them about religion. It is my hope that people will be able to draw different religions together and see that they are all divined of the same God. Monotheism. That is what they are all supposed to be about, at least the honest and real ones. I have written about them as such and hopefully get readers that have that understanding of the doctrine to converse about the books after they read them. One of the fiction books that I am writing is about people who are dead and within the Hereafter. They are going on board the Ark of the Covenant to judge people on Judgement Day. They are all excellent people. The book goes in depth into *Revelations* of the Bible. It is a really challenging book. I am at a pause in writing it and am waiting for Paige to give me some ideas for it.

Paige is a really helpful Dog for writing. When I come to a pause spot, she comes up and waves her paw at me for a treat to distract me and to bring my thoughts back to the plot. When I am done giving her treats, I usually am thought-out and ready to write again. So, she lays down with the intention of letting my thoughts process and she looks around to protect me from others... which is what she does... and I write and write. That is good of her.

And it is good of me to write. I am unemployed and am a writer for a job. It is a pleasant for me to write books. I haven't been published yet, not at the time of writing this book right now, but I am working on it. Paige is good with the writing. She relaxes when I am writing and doesn't distract me at all. She is wonderful to be around! It will be a good thing to get published, though. I want to be able to get the input from the readers on the books so that I can give them input on the criteria that I have written about. And Paige can act kindly to them if they get to meet her at the bookstore.

Overall, Paige is really kind to people. Granted, a bicyclist just came into the Coffee Shop and was saying Hi to Paige and she started to bark at him! Why? He has dogs, so figured that his dog may have bit someone or acted like it was going to bite someone, and Paige didn't like that concept. But overall, she gets along well with other people. Many of them want to pet her and say hi to her. She likes it. They don't pet her because there is a restriction on it on her sticker, but they hold their hand in front of her nose so she can smell them and hold it there for her. That is so nice of them to do! So, Paige gets along well with the people she is around, for the most part. She also smells their legs, and a lot of people have dogs that put an odor on their legs that Paige smells when she sniffs at them. She likes to sense the other dogs. Granted, when the other dogs are around, if they are not Service Dogs then she doesn't like them usually and she barks at them. But Service Dogs or other Golden Doodles she likes.

There was a guy outside the Coffee Shop that had a Golden Doodle out there that was black that stopped by with me and Paige and said "Hi" and talked about his dog. Paige liked his dog. It wanted to come inside and visit with her. It was pulling on its leash that was around the chair outside to free it so that it could go through the door to the inside where Paige was sitting. The guy finished the conversation and went outside and got the leash from the chair and the next time I looked he was gone. He was a nice guy. I have seen him in here in the Coffee Shop a lot when I am here. He usually says Hi to me and Paige.

There is a distinct difference between the beginning of this book and the middle and end of it. The beginning is written in a bizarre and abbreviated form. That was because it was initially one of the first books that I wrote after getting possession of Paige. That was a distinct difference in the format of what I was writing about, and the writing process. Before, I was leaning how to handle Paige and it took effort. So, I put the effort into my writing about her. Now, in the middle and end of the book, I have gotten used to handling Paige and have been writing more resolute editions of text to describe the handling procedures. Thus, the book improves as time progresses.

Hopefully, the editor will see that and not hold

it against me when he edits the book. This paragraph should help!

For the most part, writing about Paige is writing about her daily activities. She goes everywhere except the hospital with me, except we go there together for medicines, and she spends 24 hours per day with me, 7 days per week. She is a delightful animal! She gets along with me fantastically. Most of the time she lays down around me with her head down and her eyes open, looking around at people around me in a protective format. Sometimes she gets up and begs me for a treat. Other times she goes up and sniffs people to smell their dogs, or their Service Dogs, on their legs. But usually she just lays down. Granted, she will get up and depart the area that I am in when it is time to leave. I can say something like: "Let's Go!" and she will follow me or lead out the door. She is so good at obeying Commands that I rarely even practice with her. Granted, I should practice more with her so that she can remember them. But I forget.

In this chapter of the document I am writing down the actions of Paige as the days go on so that you, the reader who may be considering getting a Service Dog or the handler of a Service Dog or regular dog would get the idea of what handling one is like. That ways, you would be more adapted to go to the class to get a Service Dog and to handle one for your own possession. That is what this chapter is for... to help you to possess and handle a Service Dog of your own!

ANOTHER PERIOD OF TIME WITH PAIGE

Today I took Paige for a walk down the neighborhood. Down the street that runs crosswise next to our street there was a lady walking two little dogs. She walked past us as we were walking over towards her, then as we were turning around, she turned around with her dogs. She was on the opposite side of the street. As she turned around her dogs started to bolt towards Paige, barking. She pulled on the leash. As she did, one of the dogs broke free of its leash and started to run across the street at Paige without looking across the street. It could have gotten hit by a car! It stopped short of Paige's leash.

Paige accepted the dog without bolting after it. The lady came running over and called her dog and picked it up by its chest and held it in her arms. She had no other way to control it, and she had to get it out of the street. As she picked it up Paige started to try to bolt for it even though her leash was attached to the frame of my scooter. I told her the Command loudly: "Don't!" and she listened to me, but still moved from side to side. The lady walked back across the street with her little dogs and said "Thank you, I am so sorry..." to me. Me and Paige kept on walking down the usual route and got to the end, turned around, and came back.

Krishna was walking on the side of the street with Forest. She counselled him at first because he was on a really long leash and he started to walk from the house across the street without looking for traffic. "What do you think you are doing, Forest? Why are you crossing the street without looking for traffic? You could get hit... you foolish dog! What is wrong with you?" She wasn't happy with the way he was behaving, and she said something about it. He didn't listen. He ran across the street without looking anyways like he didn't care. No car or truck came by, gladly, so he didn't get hit. But they could have. And that was what worried me and Krishna.

But it was over, for the time being…

The walk was a good walk. It was really acceptable and prevalent. Granted, there were some things that the Dogs did that were in error, but overall… they did okay. The Dogs really like to go for walks, and me and Krishna like to take them for them. It is an excellent experience that they do really well at. Granted, there is often an error or two on the Dog's part, but that is because they are Dogs and not having the mindsets of people. Granted, Paige is really smart. So is Forest. And Forest is 19 years old! That is about 4 years past the average lifespan of a Dog! But he is doing really well. Paige is only 4 ½ years old. She is also in really good health. So, that plays into their ability to walk in a profound manner with effectiveness and ability. That is so nice of them to do. And it is of a Dog's nature!

Today is the 26th of January. There was a Graduation Ceremony for Canine Support Teams today. They had it at the winery down the street from me and Krishna's home. I rode there in Krishna's car with MK driving it and Paige in the back seat. Krishna went there with L in the van, separately because they needed to get gas on the way there. Me and MK didn't. There was enough gas in the car to get us there and back.

MK and I drove to the winery and pulled into the parking lot. There were a lot of cars there and tons of people walking around the front of the buildings on the sidewalk. MK stopped the car after we pulled into the turn-around and the right-hand turn and said: " you can get out here and wait for me. I am going to drive in and park the car. I don't want you and Paige to have to walk all the way from the end of the parking lot to here. So, just wait here for me and we can walk in together, okay?" He was cheery and eager to make things comfortable for me and Paige. He really wanted to be there for the get-together.

So, I sat on the bricks next to the bushes there and Paige stood up and ready to move towards me when cars came running inwards... which they did. They were cautious of her and saw her and drove around leaving space for her to keep on standing there. That was so good of them! The attention was also because there was a Graduation Ceremony between graduates of the Service Dog classes and so they knew about the residual cognizance of the Service Dog that I had. She was like theirs, or the ones that they had experience with or knew about.

After a spell I saw MK walking on the other side of the driving space. I walked over there with Paige shouting out his name for attention. He saw me and said that he was really eager to go in and see the ceremony. We kept walking. Behind him there was a lady in a mauve dress walking with a Service Dog that had a Service Dog sticker on its vest. She was walking with a group of males and females. She said to me that she was really excited to meet my Service Dog, which was back next to her dog sniffing him. I asked her if her Dog was a male, and she said it was. I don't remember the name she gave to me of it. She walked ahead of me, then, because I am handicapped and cannot walk at a normal pace. So, I followed her into the yard outside the buildings. There were fields of grass surrounded by lengths of concrete walkways. There were icons holding up umbrellas over the sitting area full of tables, and at the tables were tons of people.

We walked down the sidewalks past a building. I was showing the lady with the Service Dog the way to the classroom because I had been there the previous two years for graduations… including my own graduation during which I received a transcript of Success! I saw across the grass and walkways the front of a building with a bunch of people standing in front of the glass leading outside. I told the lady: "That is it! The front of the building probably has a sign about it there. Look! There it is!" As I said that I saw a sign hanging about the standing area against the building that had a picture of a Dog's paw in large, and it said: "Canine Support Teams Graduation Ceremony! All Service Dogs are welcome!" Very nice! That described the event in a simple but elegant terminology. I read the sign to the lady, and she saw it and said she was going over there, and we walked to the front of the building next to the glass looking indoors.

On the sidewalk on the front of the building there was a door leading to the inside that was open. Next to the door was an Entry Station staffed with members of the Canine Support Teams registering people that are signed up to attend and giving them seats. They were writing the seats down so that there was no conflict. Many of the groups had more than one person attending. The staff had to do so because the attendees had to pay to attend the event. It was doable, but it also includes the cost of the lunch that they gave to us... which was delicious.

I stood in the front and saw through the window that Krishna was coming over to me from the inside, smiling and waving her arms. As I walked into the front door and the receiving desk there were a lot of Service Dogs with their handlers walking back and forth. Paige was really curious and friendly and kept on going over to the other Service Dogs and sniffing them in the face and on the butt and all over. She was also probably putting forth a scent of "friendliness" for the other Dog to sense. They were sniffing her in kind. They were both really friendly. And she did it to multiple Dogs.

As I was walking over to the front door, I saw the Canine Support Teams Groomer that groomed Paige and Forest a little while ago. She remembered my name and said Hi to me with it. I didn't remember her name, but

I talked to her about what it was like at CST. She said that she was having an outstanding time there. Grooming the Dogs was a good passage of time, and she enjoyed it. She was able to Groom a lot of Dogs, both Service Dogs and non-Service dogs. She asked how Paige was doing, and I told her that Paige was doing fine. I said that she really got along with the other Service Dogs at the get-together and had been playing with them. She liked what I said about Paige. She was an excellent Groomer. She had done a fantastic job on both Paige and Forest. Then Krishna came outside and said hi to her. Another lady with her black Service Dog came over to us and started to talk about the Grooming of her Service Dog. She was wondering if it could be done. She had overheard me and the lady's conversation about the Grooming of Paige and Forest. So, she joined in the conversation. As she did, I told her that I had to go inside with Krishna, and she said "Ok" and I left with Krishna.

Krishna had the seating numbers because before we showed up at the convention center she pulled in and went to the counter and got the tickets for all of us who had paid for it. So, we followed her into the meeting room which was also the dining room and we sat down at a table by the front windows and down the wall from the front door. I sat in a chair that was next to a table with about 10 different settings and chairs for it. Each table was like that. The occupation area was set up for a lot of people. I sat down with Paige sitting right next to me, looking at the other Service Dogs within the area. On the table was a large aluminum dish with a plate on top of it that had salad on top of it. I tried the salad with the forks that were around it. The salad was delicious. It had lumps of blue cheese within the area of it on the lettuce. And the dressing was delightful. As I ate the salad the presentation by the staff of Canine Support Teams began.

I don't remember the name of the premier speaker. And this story is private anyways and I didn't get his name to get permission from him to put this down in writing with his name, so his name had been left out of it.

The premier speaker stood up on the stage and started to talk about the events that were to occur. Then he talked about the puppy trainers. The puppy trainers were the people who took the puppies as youngsters into their homes and trained them to become Service Dogs... a very special accomplishment that speaks of divine powers among the trainers. The man mentioned the names of the trainers who trained the Service Dogs that went to class to become handled by the students that the graduation was for. So, they deserved a good deal of credit. The Dogs that were there at the CST Graduation Ceremony had all been trained by trainers within the CST training group. Most of the Dogs there at the Graduation were handled by graduates of the previous year. But others, like mine, had been trained years before. The availability to go to the Graduation was put forth to all of us so that it was open to whatever year had graduated. We just had to pay for it.

Then a CST member stood up on the stage with a handful of Graduate Certificates in binders and gave one to each of the trainers that they called. The trainers came forwards and got a prize each for their Good Job Done!

Then one of my instructors stood on the stage and started to talk about the Prison Pups Program. That is a program where the inmates of a prison who are on good conduct and want to be rehabilitated can get the job of helping the CST members to train the young dogs… under 2 years old… to be Service Dogs. She talked about how the program operated. Then she introduced a video on the big screen of the place. It played pictures of inmates sitting in a chair or in a wheelchair, and they were in front of a Service Training Dog that was following their commands and their hand-and-arm signals and doing things for their commands. Like bring them treats or objects or shoes. Then the picture changed to a picture of the Prison Pups Program icon, which is a picture of a large outline of paw prints behind bars. That is a pure picture of what it stands for. The onset of the program is literally effective! The Prison Pups Program keeps some 99% of inmates out of jail or prison upon their release because taking care of pups rehabilitates them!

Then the CST instructor stood back up again and talked about the PAWS program. PAWS, it stands for Pups Assisting Wounded Soldiers. My Dog has a PAWS sticker on her vest. Paige is really good at helping me deal with the PTSD that I have when I have a symptom of it come out, which happens from time to time. She sees the symptoms emerge and comes over to me and really calmly licks my arm or my leg or begs me for a treat to distract me. She doesn't accept a treat when that happens. She just wants me to shake her hand and calm down. She is such an appropriate and excellent Dog. She makes it seem like there is no PTSD present.

I didn't have any episodes of PTSD at the Graduation. As I was sitting down, after the PAWS video was over, the staff took a break and turned on some music. As they did an older skinny lady came over to me. She was really talkative and really kind. She said that she had seen Paige and I come into the place and she could tell by the way that Paige kept on looking at me all attentively that she really cared for me as her owner. I appreciated the compliment. So did Paige! As she gave the compliment Paige put her paw upwards against my leg to get my attention and I shook her hand. She wanted a treat! So, I gave her one. Then she shook my hand again, she was so pleased, so I gave her another treat. Then I looked at the lady and saw the sticker on the front of her dress. It had the name of the winery that we were at with the term "Owner" stamped beneath it. So, she was the owner of the fine vineyard winery we were at! I was very proud to be brought to her attention within her compound with my Service Dog at her distinct attention! She kept on petting Paige and saying all kinds of nice things about her. Eventually, she said "Goodbye! Gotta go! So much to do!" and she left, waving at us. I said bye back to her.

Then the CST staff came back up and Carol

Roquemore, the founder of CST, started to talk about the graduates of this year's classes. She said their names and the names of their Service Dogs, the names of the Dog's trainers and the place for them to go to stand to get their Certificates. Then the students started to go up with their Service Dogs to the stage and stand next to it in order to receive their Certificates of Excellent Performance and Graduation. They deserved it, if they were anything like the students of my class. I can say that because the students of my class were excellent!

Then the staff put us on a music break. As they did an older lady came over to me and asked me if my Dog was related to another Golden Doodle that was across the way. I asked her what its name was, and she said it was named "Tahoe". I told her that the only Dogs that I knew of that were related to Paige was her brother Henry and her sister whose name I do not remember. The lady said OK, and then she went on with business elsewhere. Then the meal came.

We got a small plate of food that consisted of half a chicken over three potato halves, broccoli, and two tubers. It tasted really good. Paige was ready for me to eat. Before they brought the food, she had begged me for treats. I gave her some pup-peroni slices. Then I ate my food. I thought it was delicious, even though it was a little bit small. It didn't fill me up. But shortly after the waitresses took the plates, they brought by some dessert. When they brought by the dessert, I was talking again to the lady who mentioned Tahoe. She was asking me about my military service. So, I was telling her. I told her about how I was cared for a lot by Paige because she could treat me for the PTSD that I have. "How did you get it?" the lady asked me. I told her that I had been on deployment and was returning in 1999 when I was in Hawaii, I was told by my platoon sergeant that 7 Force Recon Marines had died on a helicopter crash off the USNS Pecos. She gasped and put her hand on her mouth, shuddering. I told her that me and my platoon had trained helo operations on that ship and were going to go back there after the incident and do it again. We were troubled by the deaths... and rehearsed after that with our PTSD the effects of what we would do on board a helo if it started to crash with us on it. Of course, there is nothing we could have done to keep from going down with it. But we rehearsed anyways. That is what PTSD is. It is the mental rehearsal of bad things happening to oneself that one tries to fix. Even if it is impossible to fix it. I told her that Paige licked my arms and legs and begged me for treats without accepting them to calm me down. And it worked! Then I told her about how I had gotten out of the Marine Corps on an injury from the Wind Tunnel in Freefall School. It had almost broken my back and leg and neck. I was still injured, and the injury stayed with me all the way through my next deployment to my next command. I was so injured that there was no way that I was going to be able to go back into Force Recon Company, so I chose that, instead of lose rank getting transferred as a staff sergeant to Headquarters, I was instead just going to get out and get another job.

The lady was really sad for me and wished me the best with my luck. She said that I was a very lucky man to have recovered the way I did from my injuries. She said that I was a glad man for having such a remarkable Service Dog. She was right about that one. She said that Paige took very good care of me. She was right about that one, too. Paige sent the idea to her mind… accurately. So, I said "Thank you" to her, and she left to go eat dessert. I turned around and ate mine. It was delicious.

Paige lay down in her spot with her head down and surveilled the other Service Dogs within her proximity as I ate the delicious dessert. It consisted of blueberries and strawberries under a cream custard and they were all held within a cup of colored chocolate walls. They tasted divine. I ate the whole thing. When I was eating it, Krishna told me about how she had seen a guy with a Service Dog that had a Doll strapped to a leash around its vest. What did it mean? She wanted me to go over there and check it out with her. So, I did, after I took Paige into the bathroom and I went pee, then I went over to Krishna and told her that I was ready to see the guy's contraption.

We went over to the other side of the table that was to the inside of our table and there was a guy sitting there. He had a vest on his Service Dog that had a doll on the buckle on the vest. It was a very small doll but had a very funny face on it. It looked like a snickerdoodle type doll. The guy saw us looking at it and said that it was amusing that we were so interested in it. It was something that helped bring by the day, day after day and it was a delightful contribution to his being. Very nice of him so say! He was laughing and laughing! The guy had it going on wholesale with his doll within his vest and made me want to get one for my Lion doll George or my Rabbit Peter to be able to go in. So, we thanked him and went back to the table.

"Are you going to get one of those?" Krishna asked me.

"Absolutely. That guy really defines wellbeing! I want to be just like him!" I responded.

So, we sat down at our table and the staff of CST started a raffle for the people there. We had a few tickets. We didn't win anything. The raffle took a long time. Paige lay down next to me and kept her head down. She was done shaking my hand for treats, so I got a break from getting her out pup-peronis. The rally had people at one table who were not winning anything, but they were waving their hands all around with each number being told out to us to distract as though they had won. I don't know what was going through their minds.

Oh yeah... when we sat down at our table to eat lunch there were a couple of other women who had come and sat down next to us. They didn't get a meal because they were vegetarian, and the meal had meat in it so they couldn't eat it. They couldn't get one made for them, though, because they were supposed to have told the staff about their dietary needs before the meal started so it could have been made for them. So, they didn't get anything to eat. It turns out that they were called to the stage a bit later and received awards for training the Dogs. They were a couple of trainers that went from location to location when the Dogs were being trained to be Service Dogs and helped to train them and their handlers. Very nice girls. I told them they did an excellent job when they returned to the table.

After the rally people started to stand up and move around the room. I could tell that they were getting ready to leave. I told Krishna and she and MK and L all agreed that it was time to go. Paige was ready to depart, too. So, we headed out. The area outside was filled full of people. We made it all the way to the car and got into it. We stopped by a honey stand that was on the sideroad on the way home and bought some honey from a beekeeper that lived in the house there. He was a nice guy, and the honey is probably delicious. He had a dog that was a non-Service dog in his house. MK went to meet him at his cart with honey on it outside by the front door. Next to the cart with the honey on it was three big windows leading into the house. I had taken Paige to the house to meet with MK by the honey farm but as I did it the other dog came a-barking and barking up a storm, putting its paws on the window in an attempt to swat Paige. Paige didn't even bark at it, so it was likely a good dog. It just didn't like other Dogs outside. So, I went to the back of the house out of sight of the other dog and we went walking around.

After a spell, MK and the beekeeper came over and said things about beekeeping. Then they said: "Thank you" and we were leaving. We got in the car and left.

Paige had walked around the beekeeper's house readily. She was ready to go home. So, when we got home, I broke out my computer and began to type. Paige lay down peacefully on her bed and put her head down like she was asleep… but I knew better than that. She was just resting. She was still awake and ready to protect me, even though there were no more Service Dogs around anymore. She is such a delightful Dog!

Well, that completes this chapter. I hope you enjoyed it as much as I enjoyed writing it! We look forwards to going to the Canine Support Teams Graduation Ceremony every year! That will be nice. I really dig those CST people!

QUESTIONS TO PAIGE ABOUT SCIENCE

(Include questions regarding George's DNA and magic)

"Paige... will you answer questions about the makings of light beams in the act of Creation? Do you understand the question? How will you show me the Answer?" I shall ask this question. Then I shall ask the question: "What was the Force of Light in the Creation of the Lion George?" I am hoping I get good answers. It will probably be restricted to Paige making a body motion that alludes to the onset of Light beams in the air, if that is where they come from!

I am asking these questions of Paige to get answers for my book titled The Elegant Lion Named George. It is about how Krishna had gotten me a Lion for the

Hospital when I was under siege by the murderer of me, recovering from my injuries and brain damage. George did a lot for me, and even though he is just a doll he has miraculous powers towards healing and commonsense items. I am asking Paige the questions about Science to get a full understanding of how her mind works, and to see what kind of tricks I can teach her to do with the questions I ask. That would be interesting! I have already asked her one day if she understood Quantum Physics and Einstein's Relativity, and for each one she raised her paw up to shake my hand! That shows me that she knows. The question is this: What will her answers be to the questions I ask about them? We'll see. We'll see!

So, let me write down Paige's response to those questions I asked in the first paragraph.

To the first question, she responded by crouching down with her butt in the rear and waggling her ears side to side. To the second question she came up and tried to give me a handshake. To the question about how she will show me the answer, she waved her head side to side and shook my hand.

Another day I asked her what communications God used to create light that does what light does, and that is to move like a particle and a wave at the same time. Paige put her back legs back like she was trying to get some balance, then waved her head to the side and waggled her ears as she moved her head forwards. That was her showing me that God had a body of light when he was in a realm of Nothing and He projected it forwards out of his body, thereby making a copy of it and propelling it with the force of Gravity and movement forwards, just as Paige was waggling her ears. Interesting.

Then she came up and begged me for a treat. I gave her a few of them for such a great answer. Then I asked her the following question: "What happens when God puts those forces into a photon?" And she answered immediately by rubbing her nose against my hand repeatedly. That was her showing me that there was a Force of light projected within the viewer repeatedly, letting them see the light being projected. So smart of the girl to say that the way she did! It gave me the immediate impression. (That is because she also has the ability to read minds. I'm just saying...)

That is how the questions began. I looked into my book by Gary Sinise at a random page and asked it the question: "Did Paige give me intelligent answers?" And my finger on the page was on the word "Divine". I turned to another page and asked the same question to see if I got it right, and the answer was: "...to be improved over time." So, she WAS intelligent, and needed me to ask her some more questions! Interesting!

I'll write some more as I think of more questions to ask and get the time to answer. As it stands now... it's dinner time!

I am wanting to take a moment to write about what it is like to be Paige's handler. I have covered the details of the daily occurrences in the parts about the daily occurrences, true. I have also written a chapter on the Commands given to her for practice of the Commands portion of the test I take once per year. I have written a Chapter about the Service Dog class that I took to get ownership of her, and it covers a lot of detail about what the course was about. And then there is this chapter, which is about the Scientific questions I ask of Paige and what her answers are. And of all, it shows that she is extremely intelligent. I can tell by the way she answers Commands, plays with our other Dog, follows me places, and answers questions about Science and being of me and her. Those are distinct and tall-ordered questions, and it is a miracle of intelligence that she is able to answer them so readily.

Paige is an excellent Service Dog to be a handler for. She responds to everything I do beautifully. I like to take her to the Coffee Shop, too. Of course, she is now wearing a sticker that says "Please Don't Pet Me... I'm Working" ... and that keeps people from petting her when they aren't supposed to make her uncomfortable that ways. So, the waitress there with a couple Pit Bulls that likes her can't really pet her anymore. She is okay with it. So is Paige! I am looking forwards to asking her more questions about science and seeing what her input and outputs are.

She is waking up the good side of me in my achievement history of doing Good for people. I am writing a whole book about her for the people in the United States population that want to purview how to achieve handlership of a Service Dog themselves. I want them to appreciate that a handler of one could write a whole story about his Service Dog named Paige and what it was like to raise her. I am certain that the book will be appreciated and happy, and Paige is happy that I am writing it!

That covers that part. More to follow about the questions about science to follow!

I am now thinking about ways to ask Paige the questions about Science. I am certain that she understands what the big words of science mean, like Gravity or electronics or superfusal emigration apparatus. Ha! Actually, that last word "superfusal" doesn't even exist in the average English dictionary, but I am giving it a meaning of the intermittent approaches of time and space through the onset of light rays that move at the ultimate speed. The superfusal element is the onset of the different light rays moving at a speed of GREATER than the speed of light… like tachyons… which DO exist (although nobody has captured one and measured a tachyon moving faster than the speed of light… but they are said to exist in scientific theories!)

On a different day Paige was in my room and I was on the bed with my computer. She was looking at me and getting ready to crouch on her back legs under her and her front legs up and beg me for food by raising her paw up and shaking my hand. She wanted a treat. But I wanted to discuss the onset of sound with her.

I asked her the question, as she was raising her paw up to shake my hand: "Paige. What can you tell me about the onset of sound?"

She put her paw down and waggled her head side to side, looking one way then at the TV. Then she showed me that she was listening to the TV by moving her ears upwards so she could hear better. So, she explained it in Dog terms that I could understand!

Then she went out of the room. I moved to the side on the bed to look at her and as I did, I made a noise with my rump on the bed and she turned her head towards me, showing me that she heard it. Then she saw me looking at her and she walked over to me and standing there raised her paw up to shake my hand for a treat. I gave her a Pup-peroni couple and she was happy. That was a reward for her understanding what I was saying about the onset of sound. She heard me and wanted a reward for showing me her perception! And she got one! Yes! That is how the Service Dog likes to be treated!

I asked Paige today to tell me about Parallel Universes. That is the theory of Universes that says that there are other Universes in existence that fly on different laws of physics within each one. She started out by begging me for a treat. Then, after she got her treat, to show me the onset of different forces in multiple universes she started to bend over and to scratch her hindquarters because she itched there. That was a showing of how the forces would interfere with one another when they changed throughout the universes. I think so, anyways.

I asked Paige: "What do you think about my DNA?" She was laying down in the side room when I did it with me in the bed with the computer. She came up and shook my hand with her paw, like she was saying that she liked it. "Do you really like my DNA, Paige?" I asked her. She raised her paw upwards and put it on the top of my lap and left it there, raised up. That was her telling me that my DNA was elegant and a wholesale experience that defies all comprehension. A delightful exposition!

I gave Paige a treat for shaking my hand. She is used to doing that as a form of begging. Sometimes she does it and when I try to give her a treat, she doesn't eat it. She had just wanted to shake my hand. She does that sometimes. This time she told me that she doesn't want any more science questions by leaving the room and going outside and sitting in the living room now. Ok. I am going to stay here and stop writing this part of the document, for now. I will find something else to do with my time.

Thank you for reading this far!

I want to ask Paige about what she thinks about other dimensions. There is a scientific theory that the higher dimensions are miniscule in size. Smaller than atoms. Smaller than the Plank length. That is extremely tiny. So, if it is so small, how does it operate at that level? I really don't know how to answer that question. The data on the extra dimensions is written in a four-dimensional space of earth… which is three dimensions of space and one dimension of time, for a total of four dimensions. All other dimensions bigger than four are supposed to be tiny in size. But they are said to have an effect on the elements of existence within this earth… like light. How it is really supposed to work, though, I don't know. I don't know! But perhaps Paige will. She is resting right now and not begging for treats or anything else but keeping her head down on the floor right now, so I am not going to ask her at this moment. But when she comes around, I will ask her and see what her reaction is to the question. The question shall be: "What do you know about the higher dimensions? Are there 10 different dimensions as put forth in String Theory? What about 26? Another number? Is this too many questions?" I shall ask all those questions and see what the answers to each of them are. I shall write the answers down here in the following paragraphs and tell you the outcome of those answers.

I went into Krishna's room to talk to her when she was sleeping about her brother going back to his hometown, some 8 hours away. Paige came in with her brother and we explained the trip to her. Then, Paige and I went to the kitchen. Paige was crouched down with her head up, looking at me. So, I said to her: "What do you know about the onsets of higher dimensions?" She immediately stood up and raised her paw to shake my hand. I shook it. Immediately she did it again. So, I shook her paw again and put my hand on my arm. She raised her head up and began to lick my fingers with her tongue. That was a message from her. It was that there was an extra "flavor" to the onset of light from raised dimensions. Higher dimensions were something that a person could taste with their science programs. That was what it meant. I was appreciative. I gave her a treat. But I had her sit down first, by giving her the command of "Sit" while raising my hand upwards in a sitting position. She did it. And I gave her two treats.

So, it was delightful that Paige could answer questions about science the way she did. She projected into my mind the summary of her explanation, in terms that were parallel related to the makings of the symbols that she sent to me. And she had sent them with discipline and strength. That was the way she operated. With discipline and strength.

I then sat at the counter in the kitchen, and Krishna's brother came in getting ready to leave for his city. He talked to me. I asked him what he thought I should talk to Paige about for the book I was writing about her. He said that I should talk about how the birds wake up in the morning and begin to sing and chant happy songs.

They communicate with each other, in a peaceful and ascertained nature. Then there are the ants. They are like birds in that they have the Global Positioning System (GPS) within their heads that allows them to sense and know the location of food within the area where they will be, or even outside that area. Then they also get to sense the direction to get there through the terrain. That allows the ants to move over lumpy ground in curved lines without becoming encapsulated within the rocks and they find their way to the food and they are able to get it, even when it is a longways away. Thus, they are able to find their way with their GPS back over the ground to the location of the hive – if they are bees – or the nest – if they are a bird or ant. That is the way it operates. Interesting, isn't it?

I said that set of information to Paige. She kept on raising her head to me and waggling her ears around and begging me for more treats, licking my hand when it was placed on my arm. She mentally sent me the images of the GPS so I knew it was there in the beasts. She also sent me a message about their navigation system that allowed me to see that they had a sense about them that allowed them to navigate to the object they desired throughout the procedure. That was so nice of her to do for me. The girl Paige is a genius that has an exceptional mental ability about her! And she puts it to work when she is communicating with me to tell me things about things that are only seen as products of the brain in action!

I am studying science online in between the times that I write. I just got an idea. I am going to talk to Paige about the science and physics issues as I read over them and see what her response is to them. Then I will write down her response here in this book. We'll see how it turns out!

I have the website on Wikipedia of Quantum Theory open. There are a lot of detailed words within the document and I am looking them up in other windows. I will put the terms here and see what Paige has to say about each of them. We'll see if it will get us back up to Quantum Theory, or if they go too far for it and fill up this chapter. We'll see!

Paige was laying down on her bed in my room. I asked her from my bed: "Paige. Do you want to tell me about the Electrodynamics of Moving Bodies? It is an Einstein theory! What do you know about Electrodynamics of Moving Bodies?"

Paige had her head laying down. She waggled her eyes upwards and looked at me. Then she put her head back down with her eyes open. She stayed there. She moved her eyes back and forth like she was looking at a moving object, but her body wasn't responding. After a few minutes she waggled her head upwards and put it forwards and to the side, looking away from me.

I imagine that was her sense that the Electrodynamics of Moving Bodies was equal to the movement of visualized bodies within the mind that one could see with one's eyes. And after looking at the visualized moving object for a spell one may begin to get the impression that the object was moving towards oneself, so one might move one's head to the side, so it doesn't get impacted. At any rate, that is what I imagined that Paige was doing to the Commands.

But now Paige was resting, so I decided to give her more Commands later. I call these statements "Commands" and to a degree they are because they warrant a response, but they are really "Speaking Science". There is a lot of science out there, though, so I am going to stick with the term Commands.

She lay on her bed with her head down for a bit. Then she raised her head up and looked my way with curiosity. It looked like she expected something from me. She kept her eyes focused on me the whole time. Eventually, I got my computer out off the desk and woke it up. I looked at the icons for the science programs I had on the internet and picked the oldest one. That was Quantum Theory. I asked Paige the following questions: "Paige… what can you tell me about Quantum Theory? What do you know about it?"

Paige lay there thinking for a moment. Then she wiggled her ears and opened her jaw up. She then began to lick her lips. That didn't do the trick, so she put her head down by her front paws and legs and began to lick her legs, cleaning herself.

That was an indicator that Quantum Theory is the movement of atoms in such a manner that they allow for the environment to be cleaned and made ready for usage. That was my determination of those effects. I could be wrong. I hope not! Paige is just laying down now with her head down and isn't even looking at me. So, if I was wrong then she would probably be doing something to show me. But she isn't. So, I am probably right!

It is complex to get a summary of a science question from page in a language that a person can understand without drawing the wrong conclusions. The sentence that is asked often contains a term or word that is engaged in how-to's and where-to-fores that are about how the word interacts with other elements of the theory. Thus, the explanation can be complex. Think about it for a moment. If a person asked about how "Quantum Theory operated", that is just a three-word question, but the answer is an answer that contains pages and pages of words to describe the operation of Quantum Theory. It is a mathematically evolved theory and thus defies common, simple and small word descriptions. And the Service Dog, when asked the question, will try to describe it in as simple a detail consequence as possible. Thus, the explanations are in body language that may not seem like anything that would describe anything other than the Total Projections of Matter and Energy within the Theory. I made those words capitalized because I am trying to get an idea across to you reader. I hope it works!

Paige's communication is based on the waggling of her ears, the motion of her head, the movement of her eyes, her feet, her body, her back, and the wagging of the tail. There are a lot of different ways she can move those different parts of her body, too. Each time she moves them it sends a message that perfuses the meaning of the question that I asked her. The thing is, when the question is something about science the answer may be something that is really complex when thought about in normal means of thought. So, to answer those questions, Paige has to allow for the thought process of the message recipient to take on the odds and ends of the message and to draw conclusions about the Parallel Meaning of the message and the question. If a question has multiple answers, then the recipient can think of those potential answers to the question, and when he or she looks at Paige answering the question, they can take in Parallels to the meaning that they ascribed to the question.

Paige plays her answer into the makings of the mindset and intelligence of the recipient! She can read minds! Thus, she can put the meaning of her words into the thinking process of the recipient and their intelligence and thus give them a wholesale answer. We will see what her answers are to me asking her questions about Einstein's Relativity book. I have a copy of it and just pulled it out of my property binder for review. Einstein supposedly had an IQ of 160, which is a Genius in the top 0.5% of the world! I am really curious into what Paige is going to come up with answers to Relativity, and to M-Theory and to Quantum Theory. Those are all complex, and I am going to have to relearn my mathematics to get them down. But I am working on it!

PAIGE'S TRIP WITH SUNSHINEY

Today Krishna took both of the Dogs out of her room. Paige was already dressed for the next trip. And what was the next trip? Krishna came into her room and left the Dogs outside. And she brought with her a cage to put the cat in.

The cat was hiding under the bed and didn't think of the cage, so she came out and climbed into Krishna's hand... then after a very short spell started to bulge at her body and move her paws out in resistance to being placed in the cage... which was a prison to Sunshiney. Sunshiny resisted and resisted but Krishna got her body into the cage and started to lock the cage shut on the top and bottom of the door. The thing is that Krishna wasn't wearing her glasses... so she couldn't see that she was leaving the locks open without knowing it. Sunshiny sensed it right away and erupted the door open and jumped out of the cage. Then she immediately ran under the bed and hid. Hissing!

While Sunshiny was under the bed I could hear Paige out in the hallway running around and putting her front paws on the door to open it. She wanted to come in to see what was wrong with Sunshiny. She was bounding up and down to get our attention. I didn't let her in, though. I went over to the other side of the bed that Krishna wasn't on and looked under it at Sunshiny.

She was walking around all interrupted and pacing upright back and forth with her head high in the air, clawing at nothing in front of her. She walked next to me under the bed at one time, and I reached in and grabbed her around the neck and picked her up. Krishna came over then and put her hands out. I placed Sunshiny into her hands and Krishna carried her over to the cage. This time, she lifted the cage upwards so that the opening was on the top... not the side... and she placed the cat in that-a-ways. I moved its paws to the inside of the cage because the cat was trying to articulate its way out of the cage and prevent us from putting her in there. She didn't succeed. We got her inside. This time, I took charge of the handles to the lock arms on the cage and there were two of them available... one moving upwards and one moving downwards. I pressed them down inside of the door and raised the locks towards the center. Then I moved the door backwards so that the locks were above the holes in the ceiling and the floor and I released the locks to flow within the holes in place and thereby locking the door of the cage.

That was what Krishna should have done in the first place if she had been smart enough to put her darned glasses on before she tried to move the cat around. Sometimes that woman is terribly foolish.

Krishna carried the cage with the wailing cat in it over to the car and she put it in the trunk where it would be out of the area of Paige in the back seat. I walked over to the car with Paige and had her sit in the back seat, out of reach of the cat. Then I sat in the front passenger seat, and Krishna sat in the driver's seat. We began to transit up to Krishna's former husband's house. He was going to watch over Sunshiny for the couple of weeks that me and Krishna were going to be out of the state on vacation.

Sunshiny was wailing miserably. We could hear her batting around inside of the cage with her paws and head. She was totally abrupt in her movements and actions. I was worried that she was going to hurt herself, after we had driven for a little while. But there was nothing that could be done to stop it. It had to be let proceed as the cat planned it inside of the cage. But the real concern was what Paige was going to do. There was a gap between the seats on the upper portion between the area that Paige was laying... or sitting... or standing... and the trunk area where the cage with Sunshiny was resting. Or, to be more accurate, it was Acting Out. Paige kept on looking up over the seat at the back of the car, moving her head around and raising up her ears to hear.

We finally, about 1 ½ hours later, got to Krishna's ex-husband's house. There he came outside to pick up Sunshiney. We gave her to him, and Paige jumped out of the car when let out of the back seat by me and went sniffing around in the back yard. She could smell other cats and dogs there in the grass. Krishna's ex-husband took Sunshiney in her box into the house, took her into the bathroom, and he let her out of the box with the doors shut. She went into the shower area and sat against the wall there.

We visited with the ex-husband for a while, talking about the coronavirus and what it means. Then I took Paige outside on her leash and with Krishna we all got in the car and went home.

I FAILED MY TEST WITH PAIGE, HAD A CLASS ON HER, THEN RECOVERED

I went to a store in the city next to ours that the Canine Support Teams instructor Max was going to meet me at. She was standing in front of the store when we got there. I am going to keep the name of the store secret in this story because of privacy concerns. I was there with Krishna and Paige and Max. We went inside.

We were put into position in the middle of a double aisle next to a counter with goodies on it and Max told me to have Paige Sit and the get Down. So, I leaned over and waved my hand upwards and told Paige to "Sit". She ignored me and kept on looking around. I told her again, and she continued to ignore me.

Max told me that she would show me how it was done so she could point out some errors I had. Max took Paige's leash and said to her in a really highly pitched voice while standing tall and waving her hand upwards, she said "Sit!" in a cheery voice. Paige listened to her and sat down! The lady told me to then give Paige a treat. So, I gave her one and said "Yes! Good Dog!" Then Max gave Paige the Command to get "Down", and she did immediately all the way down. I gave her another treat and said "Yes!". But my tone wasn't strong enough.

Max then told me that I was speaking in the wrong tone of voice to Paige. I was supposed to make the tone sound happy and cheerful, and the way I was doing it, it sounded bland. I said that I didn't have the same tone of voice as a female. Such a thing was impossible for a male to do, or so I thought. Max told me that she knew that I would get better at it so long as I put some effort into it and tried hard at it. So, I started to.

I tried again and didn't get a response. It seemed like Paige was distracted. I realized what was going on. I told Max about how that morning Paige had been in the mountains with a dog that isn't a Service Dog that was 19 years old and had to sit in the back of the van as we came down the mountains for 1 ½ to 2 hours. She had been interrupted. We stopped by the house and dropped off Forest, the other dog, then immediately came over to the shop to do the test. "So, she is very distracted. And there are a lot of people coming in here. We have failed, haven't we?"

"Yes, you failed. But I am going to give you a temporary ID card for her to last until you get certified again. Come over to the sitting area and we shall discuss your handling of her." Max was speaking really soundly but comfortably. We walked over to the restaurant sitting area and sat down at a table. There was nobody else there.

Max went over the things that didn't work. She said that she understood how the Dog got distracted, and she said that it made sense that Paige would do negative things, like not listen to Commands, if she had to do a long trip with a dog that wasn't a Service Dog. Then Max said that Paige was putting on too much weight. "If she gets overweight the trainers will remove her from being a Service Dog. Then you won't be able to take her everywhere with you anymore. You don't want that, do you?"

"No. Let me show you the treats I give to her. And I give her 1 cup of food in the morning and one cup of food at night. She eats a lot." I showed Max a piece of ½ inch pup-peroni that I give to Paige out of her bag. Max told me that that definitely wouldn't do.

"That is too big. You need to cut those down into ¼ the length. She needs small pieces. And she needs to be on a diet. For a month, just feed her ½ a cup of food in the morning and ½ cup of food at night. That will slim her down. Dogs lose weight fast. That should do the trick!" Max was resolute in her determination. "Now, let's walk a circle around the square of the store in the middle so that you can show me how Paige works with you in the company of people."

"Ok. Let's go!" We took off with me walking Paige, and Max and Krishna walked right next to me, looking at Paige and me.

We walked around a turn to the right and Paige started to sniff at the objects on the shelves. She also started to sniff at the people as they walked by in the other direction. I had never pulled on her leash because I didn't want to hurt her or cause her to bark at me. But Max counselled me on it and asked me to give her the leash. I gave it to her, and she started to walk with her hand on the short handle of the leash. Paige walked next to her. Immediately Paige started to sniff at the products, and immediately Max pulled hard upright and to the side on the leash, thereby forcing Paige to stop sniffing because she had been somewhat jerked to the side. Then Paige kept on walking without sniffing anything. She went without sniffing anything for quite a few minutes. Then she tried to sniff on a person walking by us. Max immediately pulled on her leash to the side and Paige immediately stopped. "See, you can do this too! All you need to do is stop moving the leash all gently the way you are doing it. You are too soft with it. Pull! It won't hurt her! And pull to the side. You have been in the past pulling upwards, with makes it so that she has to move her head forwards and down to prevent it. You don't want that. You want her to stop sniffing. So, pull to the side!"

That continued for the rest of the walk. We finished the walk around the circumference of the square and Max stopped at the end and told me about what she saw as a remedy to the problem of a failed test. "I suggest we have a get together in a few days and go over the commands with Paige again. She will probably do better if you aren't coming from the cabin and she isn't around the other dog. What do you say?"

"I'm up for it. Are you, Krishna?"

"Sure. What date will it be?"

"I'll call you and let you know." Max had our email addresses, so she could also email us too.

So, me and Krishna and Paige said "Goodbye. Thank you!" and we departed.

About a week later, me and Krishna and Paige got into the car without going to the cabin and went directly to the same Canine Support Teams kennel that I had had my class at three years ago. We called at the gate and let them know we were there and they let us in. We went into the classroom with Paige. There we met up with Max and a lot of the trainers there and said "Hi" to them. Max took us to a side room with a flaked fiber see-through wall looking outside and there were a couple of chairs in there and a table. It looked like a garage of sorts, with a concrete floor.

Max told me to do some tricks with Paige. She wanted

me to have her Sit, then Down, then Stay. I was to give her a treat after she accomplished each Command. So, I did it, kneeling down to give the

Commands (like I wasn't supposed to do), and my voice was not that cheery. Paige listened, though, and sat down. I gave her a treat. Then I gave her the next Command with the same errors, and she listened with hesitation again. I gave her another treat. It was natural for her to Stay, so she Stayed. She got another treat. Then Max criticized me.

Max said that I needed to be a lot more cheery and happy with my Commands so that she would want to do them. She didn't look like she wanted to follow the Commands then, even though she was. And I was to stop kneeling down to communicate with her. "That is throwing her off," said Max. "Stand tall and give the proper hand and arm signal." So, I agreed with her and noticed that she was making some really intelligent remarks. So, I prepared to go around with it again.

The next go-around I was supposed to get Paige to do the same trick. She was to Sit and get a treat, then get Down and get a treat, then to Stay and get a treat. I paid close attention to how tall I was standing and stood upright with minimal effort when I gave her the commands, instead of kneeling down like I used to do. At first, when I was standing tall to tell her to Sit for the first time, she looked at me oddly. That was because she wasn't used to me giving her Commands while standing up like that. She was used to me kneeling down to tell her with my hand and arm signal. But she corrected herself after a spell and then followed the Commands as I was standing up tall.

Then I told her to "Stay" again, and Max told me to go to the other side of the garage and to not look at Paige when I was going there or after I was there. And I wasn't supposed to look at her until after I had given her the command of "Come Here" without looking at her, then finally look at her when I said "Sit" and gave her a treat. So, I went to the other side of the garage and Paige lay there stationary as she had been told to and didn't move. That was so good of her! Then I gave her the Command of "Come Here" and she stood up and walked right over to me and stayed standing. Then I looked at her and waved my hand upwards while standing up tall and said to her "Sit". She sat right on down and I said "Yes! Good Dog!" to her and gave her a treat.

Max told me that what I had done was an excellent job.

Then Max sat down in her chair. I sat down in mine and Krishna sat down next to me. Max was sitting in a space across from us, next to the door going back into the classroom. She said that she was going to work on the Retrieval Commands with Paige. I told her that I hadn't really done them with her. I didn't think that the objects that I was trying with her were the right types of objects. So, Max pulled out a wooden rod that was about 1 inch wide and two feet long. She held it in her hand.

Max held the rod in front of Paige's mouth as Paige looked at it really intently. Paige was remembering what to do with objects that were given to her. Max held it up sideways and gave the Command "Get It!" in a cheery and happy voice. She did it a couple times, and Paige got it and opened her jaw and put her mouth around the stick. "Hold!" said Max aloud, happily. Paige held onto the stick for a few seconds then jerked her head forwards and let it out of her jaw. Then she moved her head immediately over and picked it up again. Then she did it again. Then she picked it up AGAIN. That was in error, but she was trying to correct her error. Max saw it, and she started to say over and over again: "Hold… Hold…Hold…Give it!" When she said the Command of Give It with her hand under the stick, Paige opened her jaw and let the stick out so Max could hold onto it. That was a good Dog!

Well, to say the least, at least Paige tried to accomplish the Command.

Max then addressed the issue with Paige's difficulties in training. "I am going to ask you… and you don't have to accept the offer… but I am wondering… would you like the Canine Support Teams to put Paige back into the Prison Pups Program long enough to bring her back up-to-snuff on her Commands and tricks? She is already showing some knowledge of it now, so it would probably only be about two weeks for her to be there. But you don't have to accept the offer, if you don't want it."

"Krishna, I am definitely interested in it," I said to Krishna. "What is your take on it?"

"Oh, I am definitely interested in it. You should do it, Max. We are going on vacation starting in a week, though, that will last for two weeks. Can we do it after we get back?"

Max was ebullient. "That is for sure. How about we start about three days after you return? Would that be enough time for you to get ready? All you need is to have her harness on and food for her available. Can you do it?"

"We sure can!" I was very happy. I wanted to be able to keep my Service Dog in Service Dog status.

And with that we went back inside of the classroom and said "Bye" to the Instructors there. Max pointed out to them that Paige was already starting to lose weight from the diet that she is on and has been on since the day she failed the test and I was counselled on her gaining too much weight. So, the problem is being remedied.

We departed the Canine Support Teams classroom. Next, I am going to do the Prison Pups Program with Paige. Then I am going to spend some time with the CST Instructors about the Commands. Then I am going to be tested again. I shall write about them here as each edition happens.

Now we are home.

Me and Krishna and Paige got in the car and went to PetCo to get a chew stick for Paige to retrieve. Paige got out of the car there readily and walked up right next to my leg with me holding onto her short leash to control her just in case she got into it with other dogs there. She was highly aware of the other dogs, but she didn't bark or lunge at them. She walked with us to the front of the store.

There in the front was a wood barrel and it had a good-sized chew stick in it. It was plastic and it looked like it was wood. I looked hard at the products and saw a bunch of different colors and shapes of chew toys. But I decided to get the first one. I picked it up and walked down the aisles to boxes of liver treats. They were of the same brand given to Paige as treats from Max. Max said that the livers for Dogs was extremely healthy.

Me and Krishna and Paige didn't take the livers with us because we didn't want to have to patch it in our luggage for the trip to another state. We decided to get it in the other state. So, we departed PetCo and went home with the chew stick.

When we got home, I undressed Paige and took the chew stick into the garage. I called her in there and Forest followed her. I held the stick in front of her mouth and said: "Get It!" She immediately bit her teeth around it and started to waggle her head side to side with the stick in her mouth. She was bobbling the stick back and forth. I told her "Hold!", but she dropped the stick instead. So, I told her "Hold!" And I waved my hand up. She was already picking up the stick... so the Command made no difference. So, I placed my hand under the stick engaged jaw and told her to "Give It!" She thought for a moment then dropped it into my hand. What a Good Dog!

It turns out that she mostly understands the importance of the mentioned Commands. She needs some work, though.

A few days later Krishna and Paige and I took a flight out of California to Idaho for 2 weeks. Paige was a great Dog on the airplane ride. In between the two flights to Idaho we stopped at an airport and waited to get on the next plane. I talked to a lady there that was really interested in Paige. She said all kinds of nice things about her. Then we flew into Boise, Idaho, and landed. We got out and went to the rental car place and got a car and took it to the hotel we were staying at.

As soon as we got into the hotel, I fed Paige dinner and then took her outside to go to the bathroom on the grassy area next to the hotel. She only peed out there. That was expected, because she was on a diet of lesser nutrients as I am writing this part of the book. I took her back inside the hotel room.

I told her to Sit, and she did immediately. I got out a treat and gave it to her. Then I told her Down, and she went down, and I gave her a treat. Then I told her to Stay, and I gave her a treat. She stayed, as I walked to the other side of the room, to the opposite side. Then I turned towards her and said to her the Command of: "Come Here!" She stood up immediately and ran over to me. I then told her to Sit and she sat down and automatically got into the Down position. I gave her a treat. Then I told her: "Up!" while waving my hand upwards, and she got up and stood in an upright position and got another treat. That was very obedient of her! It was nice that she was following all those Commands!

That concludes that day. The rest of the time was spent resting.

The next day I brought out Paige's chew stick from its pouch and told her to: "Come Here". I held the stick in front of her as I had done a few days ago when she got it and I gave her the Command of: "Get It!" This time she looked at it and kept her jaws flexed shut and didn't take it in. I gave her the Command a few different times, even pulling out a treat and holding it about the chew stick to entice her. It didn't work. She tried to get the treat without earning it. Then it dawned on me… the last time I did the trick with her and she actually got the chew stick in her jaw, I didn't give her any treats. So, she was expecting me to ignore her. So, she wasn't doing the trick now. I didn't know what to do. So, I gave her a treat and tried again. She still didn't chew on the stick. And she didn't Hold it, either.

So, I put the stick away and let her rest. It was late in the day anyway and after her dinner time, so she was tired and not interested in doing any tricks.

The third day we were up there we went on a drive some 145 miles away from the hotel. We saw a group of giant waterfalls and it was miraculous. While we were there, a lady was getting into a car with a brown colored tiny dog. She came over to me and Paige and asked if she could introduce her Dog to Paige. They liked each other, a lot! He kept hopping up and putting his paws on Paige's body and Paige kept on sniffing him. The lady said he weighed 50 pounds. She asked how much Paige weighed. I told her that she was a big 95 pounds big! The lady shook her head in wonder. We carried on the conversation for a while, then she thanked me for my time and went back to get into her truck. That was a good time, it was! And I really liked her Dog. She said that it was a Golden Doodle, too! The same as Paige. (Just smaller and only 1 year old).

We got back at the hotel room without feeding Paige in the moving rental truck for 1 ½ hours past her dinnertime. I fed her as soon as we got to the hotel, then I got her dressed and took her out to go to the bathroom. She peed first, sniffed at the ground for a ways, then pooped. I picked it up with a little dog poop baggie that I carry a bunch on with me and threw the used bag away in the trash can. Then we went back upstairs.

There we went back over the Commands of Sit, Down, and Stay, followed by a Come Here and a Sit and an Up. She did them all readily. So afterwards I began to type on the computer while Krishna read her map of Idaho on her bed. Then we went to sleep.

The next day we began a trip to Coeur d'Alene Idaho to look at places for Krishna to buy when she retires from the VA Hospital in about a year or so. The trip was about 6 ½ hours long. So, there were no tricks with Paige. Too bad…

We spent all our time in Coeur d'Alene driving around looking for a place to move to. So, all the driving meant little to no playing with treats with Paige. That did little to nothing to get her ready to be tested again when we got back, and it did nothing to get her ready to go to the Prison Pups Program again. We were up there for a week and a half. Then we drove back to Boise and went to the airport.

When we were sitting in the airport, an airline attendant guy came over to us and said that I had a really excellent looking dog. I thanked him, and then he asked me if she had ever gone barking at another dog. "You've been in here a couple of weeks ago and your dog was barking at another dog." The guy then went on to say that a kid had complained to the staff of the airport that I had a dog that was trying to bite their dog and was barking at it and he was really scared. "If your dog does that again here, you are going to get kicked off of the airline. So, stop it from doing that again."

The fact was that I remembered what had happened. The lady and the kid with the little dog they had had sat right in front of the walkway to get off of an airplane with the dog in the aisle. It was only about 5 feet away from the door to the aircraft. As I was walking, on my rollator with Paige's leash in my right hand I passed next to that other dog on my left. It was barking and barking and jolting like it wanted to bite and sic Paige. She saw it doing that and she reacted. She barked and moved like she wanted to sic the dog back. That was normal for a dog to do. I pulled on the collar and told her "Don't!" and she relaxed on the leash. But afterwards, the kid went and complained about us to the staff there. What a horrible kid. HIS dog was causing the trouble! Why didn't that oaf get counselled on his appointment book like I did for his unsavory behavior?

We got on the plane and went home. When we arrived there my roommate watched the news. It was going on about the coronavirus, which was affecting the whole USA. I was concerned about Paige, because even though dogs can't catch the disease of coronavirus, they can still get pet by people that have it and they can spread the disease that ways to me – and I really didn't want that. So, we tried to keep Paige away from other people. And the stores were all starting to close because people all had a Stay at Home order from the government to do that was keeping them from shopping. So, I wasn't going to the Coffee Shop because it was closed now. I was forced to stay at home with nothing to do but write books and watch TV and read my new book. That was okay. I also spent my days doing tricks with Paige and giving her treats for accomplishing the tricks at hand.

So, that pretty much sums up what occurred after Paige failed her test. The coronavirus struck and changed everything. And I am now up to a publishing length of this book. I shall write the rest of the chapters and work on getting it published.

PAIGE'S HEALTH

Forest's ear became infected for some reason. It was probably because of old age. As far as Paige goes, her ear was fine, so she didn't catch whatever it was that Forest had wrong with him. It didn't seem to be contagious. The real question, in-regards-to Paige's health, is this: what will her health be like over time?

It has been sound, to date, and I hope that it is okay in the future. She had coughed from time to time, though, but not a lot and only once in a while. She hasn't caught the flu or a cold as far as I could tell, not at all for the last 2 ½ years that I have had her in my possession. She has been very healthy and a happy dog! I want her to be able to stay that ways.

Today I had to remove some lint from her ear fur from some slovenly plants that were binding themselves on her fur. They were small, circular, and abrasive in construction. I had to pull them from her fur roughly, and she let me do it even though it was uncomfortable, because she knew that they were bad for her. She could sense their negativities. I pulled them free and some of the fur came loose on them as I did it, but Paige kept calm and didn't jerk free of it. That was good of her! So, I got them all free and took them to the trash with Paige following me and threw them into it, so that they wouldn't be free to get swept up into Paige's fur again on the ground. They were in the trash can, where they couldn't come free.

I want Paige's health to be solid for her whole lifetime. I want her to live to be at least 15 years old, too. I am concerned that she will catch cancer, because I have cancer and I don't think it is communicable, but I could be wrong. I don't know if it can spread to Dogs from humans. I don't know. But if it turns out that Forest has cancer, then it may be possible that the disease can spread from humans to dogs… because it may have happened in that case.

Right now, Paige is 4 years and 8 months old. I have had her in my possession for 2 ¾ years now. She has been in good health the whole time. I have met her trainers who had her in the first two years of her life, and they didn't tell me anything about any health problems that she had. So, she likely had none of them. That is good. I want a healthy Service Dog!

Paige's mentality towards health is hard to tell. But she is a happy Dog, that I am sure of, so it may be that her mind is moving in the positive nature of Good Health and Happiness that allows her to exist in such a state. That would be a good thing. It makes me wonder what it is going to be like in the Hereafter with her there! Would she help my health with positive mental outlook on it? Would she bring me to a wonderful condition of happiness and elegance? I think she would! She is already doing it now! I enjoy being around her and going places with her. And that means a lot, considering that I have taken her almost everywhere that I have gone to in the last 2 ¾ years! And I haven't caught a cold or anything within the time that I have had Paige. I have been healthy. I bet that she has something to do with that health!

Now, let me talk about the actual mechanisms for good health. It will include the methods of disease control and health of the minerals within the body of the recipient of cells and germs and diseases. It will cover how such negative things are prevented, and what the mechanisms for such a thing are. That raises the question of this… what are the elements of disease prevention that there are out there within the cells of the body? How do they work? What are diseases constructed of and how do they work? I shall answer all these questions with intelligence and deep thought and research online. Then I shall put the answers here in this chapter in this document. All those things have to do with the Health of creatures, including that of Paige. And that is what this chapter is all about!

DISEASES AND INFECTIOUS AGENTS

Viruses, bacteria, fungi, protozoa, and helminths. Those are the list of the five categories of infectious agents... or disease generators... that there are in life.

Viruses are tiny little critters that are not even critters. They are smaller than a critter can be. They are so small that they moved inside of cells and construct copies of themselves within the cell body out of the cell's frame and materials. Its core can also be used to construct a copy of a virus. They are resilient and flexible throughout.

Man, there is enough data available online to describe the onsets of viruses that there is no need to go into the regular details here. You can look it up yourself on your computer and dial in the search of "viruses and infectious agents" and you will get summaries online of the different elements on webpages of the data. So, I will let you search for the data. I am going to instead talk about how the infectious agents are stalled or halted by the onset of DNA and the genetic effects of the cells of the body. Those are what stops the infectious agents from being infectious!

So, what do those infectious agents do to become infectious? They make copies of themselves, or they halt the production of antibodies in the body or stop the movement of the cells from one part of the body to another. They do so because they want to copy themselves in order to make replications that can bring more negative data to the body system. The construction of the copies is such that they allow the copies to interrupt cell matter and take over the neurons and protons and electrons of the body in such a bad manner as to allow for them to use parts of that matter to break-apart from the cell structure and to transform into a copy of the bad infectious matter. There is a machine within the infectious matter that allows for a copy of the body parts of the infectious matter to become copied and reproduced.

So, based on what I know about the body, what is the mechanism used to prevent the infectious matter from being infectious?

There is a DNA molecule within the body that can have the precursors to infection prevention within it. The structure of the DNA parts... the code... can have programming events about it that combine with the structure of the cell parts that the infection are using to copy themselves and thus place in there parts of it that defy the ability for the infection to perfuse. That is the way it works. I would take up a picture of a DNA cell online and an infection component online and put in this file a picture of one preventing the other from occurring... but there is no internet access here at the Coffee Shop where I am located right now. So, I won't be doing that. You could probably type it into a search engine if you have internet access and do it yourself.

Paige has the genetic equivalent of antivirus applications among her DNA composition. She doesn't catch colds. At least, she hasn't shown any evidence of catching a cold during the whole 2 ¾ years that I have had her. So, that tells me that there is something the mechanisms of antivirus agents within her body that are working on a daily basis, all day long! That is good of her to do. I wonder if there is a mechanism within her mind that allows her thought process to do things and think things that allow for the structure of the antiviruses to work against viruses and germs the way that they do. She has no diseases, none of the five infectious bodies mentioned herein have been present in her. There must be something in her that is bringing her closer to Good Health!

It could just be the way she works, too. I haven't caught any colds or germs within the last six years... other than getting salmonella from bad restaurant food back in 2015. That was the only bad thing that has happened to me for 6 years. That means a lot. There is something within my body that is preventing the onset of viruses and infections from happening. I think it is within my DNA. It must just be the way that I am constructed that plays a part in the prevention of infections. It is bizarre. I am in good health after the negative onset of damage that I experienced from being a victim of vehicular homicide in 2013. I have recovered a lot from it. And I have gotten Paige in the process!

Paige is an excellent Dog! I think that she is a great help with me keeping the Good Health about me, because she does it to herself and passes the traits onto me! That is so nice of her! I am sure she has it within her brain to know how to do such a thing. She is a really intelligent Dog. She plays with Forest a lot and does things to play with him like crouch down on her front legs in front of him like she is getting ready to pounce on him… laughing. She is so funny! He paces back and forth when she does it, excited. He wags his ears from side to side and bends his head forwards. He enjoys it! Forest loves to play! Even though he is 19 years old. Man, that is an old Dog!

Paige is only 4 ¾ years old. I hope she lasts until she is at least 15 years old. There was a lady in the Coffee Shop today that told me that she had a dog and that it had died yesterday. It was 14 years old and had a tumor and a bad hip and couldn't walk right. It is my care that Paige doesn't put her paws up on things standing up and over-flexing her hips… because doing so can cause them to become dislocated and cause them to do things like break at the hip joint. I don't want that to happen. She is such a happy Dog and I don't want her to face any trauma that removes her ability to be without pain and in a healthy lifestyle.

Me and Krishna even took to go to PetCo and buy a walkway that folds up and fits in the van that Krishna has. That ways Paige can ride in the back of the van and when it is time to get out, she will wait in the back as we open the trunk of the van. We can then take the walkway and unfold it and place one end on the side of the platform that Paige was resting on and the other side on the ground, and she can walk down it to the earth without spraining her hips or putting too much pressure on her legs. That is so healthy for her. See… me and Krishna are watching out for Paige's health too! And we do a really good job of it, as you can see here with this description of the fantastic thing that we do for her!

Overall, Paige's health is controlled in a good way by the onsets of her DNA making anti-infection agents. That is a prime factor in her prevention of infections and diseases. And she has no tumors, no brain injuries, or organ displacement, no fungi or bacteria or viruses, none of the infectious matter within her body. Granted, she sneezes sometimes, but that is a natural predicament of inhaling air that has particles and atoms within it. At least it is not diseased.

I am concerned for her, though. I have cancer, see. I am concerned that she will develop it from my sickness and start to die from it. I hope not. She is a good Dog and deserves better than that! It is my hope that she lives a full life and doesn't die until she is at least 15 years old! That would be nice! And I would be 55 years old then. That is getting up there. She likes me being old, though. And she likes me being an author. She likes it when I read her parts of what I am writing about. She is such a good Dog!

I hope that writing good things about her will help her health out. I am sure it will because my will is strong. And it is my Will that Paige stays in good health and takes it upon herself to cure all illnesses and becomes strong and protective! That is her nature... and that is what I will upon her!

What can I say about Paige's health that can't be looked up online? I can talk about the irregular elements of health. Like, for example, how Paige's Soul operates with her body to make it a healthy being. That is something that could probably be found online, but not in a section about a Service Dog.

Perhaps I should read some of the books about Service Dogs. There is a book about Service Dogs that goes into how they help with people who have PTSD. Paige has learned how to handle PTSD from being a member of PAWS for Wounded Veterans. They teach the Service Dog how to handle and react to someone that is showing signs of a PTSD episode with their actions or speech or temperament. And it works, too. I have PTSD from the time in Force Recon when 7 Force Recon Marines died in a helicopter crash next to the USNS Pecos in the Pacific Ocean. That was a year after we had done the same exact drill, and from their deaths I got into the habit of rehearsing on the helicopters that I rode on the practice of what I would do if I was getting ready to die from a crash. A lot of the exercises were unrealistic... but the trauma of the possibility of death that we could do nothing about played a big role in it. I still have that PTSD. But now I have Paige, and she is trained to handle people with PTSD in ways that make it alleviated. And she is really good at it! I have had a couple PTSD episodes since I have had Paige, and each time she senses it and comes over and licks my arm or leg to calm me down. And it works fantastically! God bless her fantastic Soul!

I think that Paige acts like an Angel. She definitely has a Soul. I know that there are some people who think that Dogs can't have Souls, but they are mistaken! Dogs CAN HAVE Souls! Look at the magnificent way they handle people and events in their lives. And the way that Paige can sense my PTSD episodes is a remarkable display of her Soul's possession of upper senses. It is an amazing thing that she is able to read over my expressions and the looks in my eyes and my mouth and chin and nose and see them flex in a bad way that illustrates nothing other than the fact that I was having errant thoughts about death and dismemberment in my mind and it was wanting to get out of my head! But it couldn't, not until Paige came over to me and showed me her very kind Soul face and licked my arm, thus giving me the sense that she was there with the feeling of it and that she cared for me. Think about it for a moment.

A Dog can't care for a person without a Soul being present, can they? Not in a real way, they can't! Thus, Dogs have Souls indeed!

(That was a multiple-negative sentence. The real sentence should be: "Dogs can care for a person because they have a Soul present in their beings. That is genuine. Dogs have Souls!")

Paige's Soul is an elegant one. She has such a kind demeanor and well-being about her that it defies all expectation. She is always in Good Health, too. So far, she hasn't caught any diseases or even a cold. Granted, she coughs sometimes, but it isn't because she is sick. It is because there are molecules in the air that affect her lungs from the dust on the ground and on the cabinets. So, overall, Paige is in really good health. I am glad for her to be in such good health. She is an excellent Dog and deserves to be well-cared for. I hope that I am doing enough for her. She is resting on the floor in the Coffee Shop next to me right now as I am writing this. She knows when to relax and to rest. That is part of her Soul… Knowing When to Do Things! And she is Good at it!

She knows that I am writing when I am at the Coffee Shop. I am an author who is working on multiple books right now at the same time. This is one of those books. So as not to interrupt me, she is stationary and laying down on the floor next to me on the leash which is attached to my belt. She is in a position that looks like she is sleeping, but she is not sleeping. She has her eyes open and is looking around at passers-bye so that she can take a protective position if need be. She is a very protective Dog, with protective habits, and she does things that help her protect me whenever we are out in public. I am so happy for her being in Good Health! I definitely want my Service Dog to be able to protect me as needed from negative characters that would assault me or Paige. She will bark at either party. Even people who just made the body motion as though hitting me or her would be something they were even THINKING about! She will bark at them and lunge like she wants to strike them and bite them! That drives them away because she is a big dog and nobody wants to get bit by a big dog, and especially not one that is wearing a Service Dog sticker on her vest!

Being protective probably helps her maintain a good sense of Health about her, too. The mindset behind that is to have her body in a positive location to protect against me being assaulted, or her being assaulted, by lunging at the person doing it and biting at them. To do so she has to draw hard on the collar to drag me to the location of the bad person as she lunges for them on her hind and forefront legs. It takes a lot of effort and strength to do it, too. But she stays prepared, constantly looking at the people around me. I am convinced that Paige can read minds. There have been a few people who she has barked at that didn't hit me but were thinking about it.

I could tell by thinking the question to them: "Were you just thinking of hitting me or Paige?" And they always answer with a "Yes" expression on their faces, or they say something that is similarly a parallel to a "Yes". So, they are proving that Paige can read minds. And I am using my intelligence to interpret their expressions as being either a "No" or a "Yes" or a "Maybe". They could be any of those three. Those are the main expressions that people have to positive or negative questions.

So, maybe I have the ability to read minds to a degree, too! I am not going to prove it for this book though. Forget I said it. Just remember what I said about Paige, though. I am certain that she can read minds!

Paige's health is really excellent. She is a well-bred Dog. And she has been well cared for over the years. Her trainers that made her a Service Dog were at the Canine Support Teams student get-together where all the students from previous classes were invited to attend with their Service Dogs. The trainers and instructors and the CEO of the Canine Support Teams was there as well. They were putting on a show for the students and a sermon for the graduates. It was really nice. The previous trainers of Paige sat next to me and Krishna and talked to us about raising the Dogs. They didn't say anything about Paige getting sick or coughing or anything like that. I am sure it is because she has always been in Good Health! Either way, the conversation was really nice. I learned a lot about what it is like to raise young puppies and get them ready for their owners.

When Paige was very young, she used to bite and eat everything she could clamp her jaws on! She ate yard furniture, couches, chairs, stools, food bags, but not trash bags. She would chew through them and snip at their cores and bite holes through them and such. Rude but playful! The trainers would take the bitten object away from her and tell her the Command of "No!" or "Don't!" and have her sit down. It worked, too! She learned those commands and still does them to this day! Nice! And she doesn't bite on the furniture, either! So, Paige learned, and it has made her a calm and wholesale Dog ever since!

Her initial trainers asked me how her health was. I told them that it was really well. They were happy! They said that she deserved to be in Good Health, and I agreed with them. I want her to be and to stay a happy Dog! A Healthy Dog!

Now let me tell you about the higher elements of Paige's health.

Let me tell you about the normal reactions that Paige had to objects around her.

She stands up tall and steady. She has long legs and a tall demeanor to her. She stands upright with her body and keeps it flexed a little bit forwards so that it can help her move her head around to see better. She has a sound neck that allows me to put a collar on it to walk her around. The collar that I got for her is a brace collar with links of metal that have edges to them going towards the skin. It is not to punish her, because the brace that links the links together has a buckle that will come unbound if there is too much pressure put around the collar. So, there is not too much pressure put on it to choke her. And she knows that the collar is a safe one. She enjoys getting into it! Her neck goes into it readily and doesn't budge any. As far as her body goes, when I go to the Coffee Shop or out of the house, anywhere, I put on her the collar and a vest around her body. Let me describe the vest.

The vest has two loops on it. One goes around her head and the other look gets strapped around her body with a buckle. The body of the vest is camouflaged in Marine Corps garb. On one side there is a sticker that says: "Canine Support Teams – providers of Assistance Dogs". On the other side is a sticker that says: "Please Don't Pet Me – I'm Working" around a picture of a hand with a do-not symbol placard stenciled over it. And in the middle is a sticker that says: "PAWS – For Wounded Veterans" with a picture of an outline of a man in uniform saluting and standing next to a Service Dog at attention. The vest is one layer deep and goes around the outer portion of the chest of the Dog. It is designed so that if one wants to, one can probably have pouches stitched to the sides of it to carry treats in it.

Paige has no problem carrying the weight of the vest. She wears it everywhere that we go outside of the house. She is sound in her bodily construction. Everywhere I go with her she had on both her collar and her vest. They don't obstruct her movement or her ability to walk readily. She had never stumbled with them on, never fallen, and never had abbreviated footsteps. That is because she has the strength within her body to carry them all wholesale with little to no effort. That is such a good thing of her to do. It makes me very proud of her.

That is an indicator that her health is really good.

Another indicator is the movement of her head when she stands or walks. I can see her eyes, even under the curls of her hair around them, and I can tell what she is looking at. I can see her pupils. At night, when I am in my room working on my computer from the bed next to the TV, Paige stands there ready for a treat and moves her head towards the TV sideways. Then she rotates her eyes over to the TV set and watches the screen. She lifts up her ears a little to hear the sound of the people talking on the Cooking Channel a bit better. She sees them cooking food, and it makes her hungry. But hunger was why she came over to me anyways. So, at that, she looks over at me, rotating her head in my direction, and she raises her paw up to shake my hand. That is how she begs for a treat. She has been taught the very cordial way of shaking my hand when she wants something to get my attention. And she looks me in the eye when she does it, in a manner to explain that she: "Really wants my attention…I am shaking your hand… so GIVE ME A TREAT!" Her eyes explain that message. So, I give her a treat out of my pouch of treats that I keep around my waist on a belt. It had a plastic bag with Pup-peroni slices in it for her to eat. She likes them. But my point is that overall, the movement of Paige's head and eyes and ears is relevant to her stature and body position and capable of helping her to do the things that she senses must occur.

I can tell the pulse of Paige by looking at the skin under the fur of her nose. If there was an error in her pulse, it would show by putting up a frequency of the upper pulse to show along the edges of her fur on her nose. That is how it would work. The fur on her nose has blood going into them in the cores of them and the blood flows in part through the veins and arteries of the body of Paige. The bloodstream leaves a signature. It is that signature that I have determined that I have the capability of seeing upon my vision of Paige's body. That is how it works. And it is profound. It is thus that I can read Paige's health rate and tell, by the flow of her blood, whether she is in good health. And Paige right now is in excellent health!

So, as I have put here, I have a distinct knowledge of Paige's well-being. All the elements of knowledge of how she is doing have been covered herein.

Today is in December 2019. Paige didn't eat her food that was placed in her dish this morning and she started to bobble her head around side-to-side. Krishna took a look at her ears and kept on asking her what was wrong with her. Paige kept on panting... a lot. We couldn't figure out what was wrong with her. Krishna thought that she had something stuck in her throat. So, Krishna kept on asking Paige to show her her throat. Paige refused to. So, Krishna thought there was something seriously wrong with her. I had to keep on telling Krishna that there was nothing wrong with Paige... that she was just sick and going about it normally. But Krishna would hear none of it and decided to take Paige to the vet in another town.

We drove all the way there and Krishna said that what she was worried about was how her dog named Lucky had been going through choking spasms. She took him to the vet and he died there. She was worried that the same thing was going to happen to Paige. She kept on looking back at her while driving to see if she was choking. I didn't even look because I could tell that there was nothing we could do if she was. We were on our way to the vet anyways.

When we arrived at the vet's office the lady at the front counter said that they couldn't serve us because they were in the middle of an operation. Surgery. So, we asked her if she could look at Paige and tell us if she saw anything wrong with her. She said she could see that she was panting and if she hadn't eaten any treats then she needed to go to the emergency room. She gave us the address there. She said it would cost $100 to go for a review. We decided to not go. And we instead went and took Paige with me to the Coffee Shop. When we got inside, I didn't give her any water because it appeared that she didn't want any. But she begged me repeatedly for treats, so I gave her some Pup-peroni sticks. She was happy. She was recovering excellently.

I got picked up form the Coffee Shop some two hours later. I got taken to a restaurant that served Lamb Shanks and rice that was delicious. I ate ¾ of the lamb and gave the rest to Paige. She was hungry, and she ate it up readily! It was on a whole bone. I took the bones away from her so she wouldn't choke, and we left.

So, Paige was not too sick. She recovered really readily. In the space of three hours. That was all it took. She is a Dog that is in really good health. I enjoy her company, too. She is a fun Dog to be around!

Paige is a really intelligent Dog; she is she is! She plays with our Burmese Mountain Dog/Border Collie mix with fun and excitement on a daily basis on her own with no recommendations from any of us people to it. She does it on her own! That is so good of her! She shows a kindness to the other dog (he is not a Service Dog so I am making his name "dog" in lowercase, while Paige's is in Upper Case because she is a Service Dog). She gets along with him really well. That is a good thing for her to do. What else is there to say about her intelligence?

She plays tricks readily and understands what the Commands are for her to listen to. When she hears a Command, like "Sit", with a hand and arm signal attached to it, then she immediately pauses what she is doing, waggling her ears to show she was listening. Then she stops doing whatever thing she was doing and sits down with her front paws erected up and her back paws bent under her body. She is such a kind dog! She often waggles here ears when she does it to sense whether or not there are more Commands to follow the initial "Sit" Command. And I can tell what she is doing. I pay attention to it. And I notice her actions are part and parcel to her beliefs that such a thing should occur. It is processed as such within her brain. Thus, her capability to follow Commands and to understand what they are and mean verbally is an indicator of her extremely high rated intelligence!

She interacts with Forest our other dog a lot. Sometimes she wants to draw him into playing with her so she crouches down readily on all four paws like she is getting ready to pounce on him and keeps her head raised upwards so that she can stay in the sic-'em position. That does the trick and draws him to waddle around side-to-side getting ready to be pounced on. And it gives her attention for her antics. That is so funny! Whatever could be going through her head to do such a thing? I know that she is thinking that she is going to get in that position… just raises the question of this: "What is going through her head when she does it?" I don't know. I just know that it is really funny!

More about Paige's intelligence… She shows how intelligent she is by communicating with her body motions. When she thinks about something moving from point a to point b, she moves her head from side-to-side in a smooth and elegant fashion. That is her showing the sense of motion.

When she wants to hear something, or to draw one's attention to a sound that she hears, she moves her ears upwards. That puts them in the physical location of being able to get more sound waves underneath them because they are raised upwards. That is a good indication that she is trying to hear something. The other indication is that if she can hear something, then so probably can you, the person. Thus, when she moves her ears about upwards to hear better, or sideways to adjust the volume of the sound, then that is also her saying to you, the person, to listen carefully at the sound that is coming out. And that capability of listening is also an indicator that the Dog wants the person to notice where the sound is coming from and to potentially do something about it. Possibly. There are a lot of different options to sound. The Dog puts forth those options with the movement of its head and ears and jaws and neck. It can take steps towards the noise if it wants a person to do something about it, like make it louder or stop. There is a lot of things that a Dog can do when there is noise to bring to attention the makings of it.

Canine Support Teams, Inc. helps with Paige's health.

Today Krishna and Paige and I pulled up to the gate on the road to the Canine Support Team, Inc. compound. The staff knew we were coming at that time because I had told them on the phone earlier in the day, so they opened the gate on a remote control for us to come in. Krishna drove in and parked the car next to the classroom. On the other side of the car was the Dog kennel that Paige used to stay in when I was a student there. There was Dogs barking from the kennel. But I think that Paige could sense that they were Service Dogs... so she was calm and didn't bark back at them!

Krishna and Paige and I went inside the classroom. Carol was sitting on her wheelchair at the front desk. She welcomed us in and said: "Merry Christmas!"

"How are you doing, you two?" There was Carol and another older lady in a black shirt standing there. "Pleased to see you all! Here!" I handed them presents for them. One was for the Canine Support Teams (a box of chocolate cookies!) with a filled-out card attached, and the other present was in a box in a bag for Carol. There was a card attached to that one as well! "Here's your presents. I hope you enjoy them!"

"Thank you much," the two of them said. We continued on with our conversation. They asked how Paige was doing. I told them she was doing remarkably well. They asked what her brother's name was.

"Henry! It is Henry! I remember because he was in the same class that I went to." I was pleased to know her brother.

Then another lady came in and had all kinds of good things to say about her. "But there is a problem with her,"

I told the lady. "She likes Service Dogs and is always kind to them... but non-Service Dogs she barks at and moves like she wants to sic them! I don't know what to do about it!"

"She shouldn't be doing that. After all, she IS a Service Dog! She can be trained otherwise. Give her to us for a spell and we will train her." Carol was sure of that. And I was grateful. I had the idea but not the knowledge that the CST trainers knew how to stop a Dog from being belligerent. But they did. That was Good!

Krishna departed into the other room with the first woman, and there Krishna bought us tickets to the 2020 Graduation Ceremony. There are tons of Service Dogs at those meetings and Paige really enjoys them... a LOT! During the last one she got to see Henry and her sister too (whatever her name is... I don't remember). It was told to me that we had tix now. I was sooooohappy!

When Krishna came back out there were two more women out there, for a total of 4 plus Carol. The two new girls said that they did Dogsitting and grooming at an affordable price. And they loved helped us clients! Krishna likes it and agreed to get Paige groomed tomorrow!

This is tomorrow. Today me and Krishna took Paige and Forest to see the CST trainer that was going to groom them. She said that she could groom Forest as well, just for a mere bit more than Paige. We left them there for her to take, and we went and drove to the Coffee Shop for me to write some while waiting for them to get groomed.

About 3 hours later we were at the mall and we called the CST headquarters and they said that Paige and Forest were done being groomed. So, we drove over there and called them on the phone and got let right into the gate. We went inside the classroom to an office in the back where the trainer was making some paperwork for us for the grooming. They had two little dogs in there that were being trained to be Service Dogs. They were such nice Dogs! And they didn't show us Raven, the Dog that was about 8 months old that was being trained to be a Service Dog that Paige got along with really well the previous day. She was a little black Doggy that was small! Then we got taken out to the kennel where Paige and Forest were waiting for us.

In the kennel there was a Dog that kept on barking. The trainer said that he was not going to be accepted as a Service Dog. There were other dogs that they had that were not going to be accepted either. Two other ones. They had development issues. Too bad. They would have liked to be Service Dogs… they just were unable to do the tricks. But Paige and Forest got along with them really well. They were waiting for us to take their vests out and put them on them and attach their leashes to them so we could drive them around. We did that and they came out already to go! They didn't bark or anything, either! They were highly calm and clean and ready Dogs! Nice!

The trainer told us that if Paige was barking at another

dog that she wasn't supposed to do that. "The trainers could train her to avoid doing that" she said. That was pleasant to hear from her. I wanted Paige to stop barking at other dogs and I didn't know how to make her stop. I had tried to tell her the Command of "Leave It!" while tugging on her leash to bring her collar around her in an effort to make her stop trying to dodge and sic the other dog. It only somewhat works. She still tries to move like she wants to sic them even when I do it. It is horrible. But I have control of her because the leash controls her movements somewhat. It could be more, though. I am wanting the trainers to do their thing to program her not to do that sort of thing. I don't know how they do it. There is some sort of way it occurs, though. That is what the trainer told me today.

We finished the conversation with the trainer, and she said "Goodbye" to us. We got in the car with the Dogs and we drove through the gate. The trainer had gone inside and had opened it for us so we could leave through it.

We went on home and the Dogs were groomed so well that they were shiny and neat-looking! That is a solid apparatus that the lady that is a CST member and trainer did for the Dogs! I also really enjoyed her company. She is a really intelligent girl!

It was good for Paige's health to be groomed so kindly!

Krishna says that Paige is getting fat from all the Pup-peroni that she eats. I don't see it. She looks at her same healthy weight to me. And she doesn't eat any more than she originally ate in the first place. So, no... she is NOT getting fat!

I am still giving her Pup-peroni treats when she begs for them. Per the CST trainers, I am not supposed to give her a treat unless it is for a reward for her proper actions. So, I have started to tell her to do things like "Sit" or "Down" to make her earn a treat. She has been doing them. So, she gets treats for it! That is good of her to do!

Paige gets told to do tricks now before she gets her treats. She has learned that that is how it is supposed to occur. So, she listens to the Command, gets it in her head that the Command is the thing to follow to get a treat, she follows it then holds out her jaw in a way that allows me to put the treat in her mouth to eat. That is so nice of her to do. That is in the frequency of training for her. It is a good thing for Paige to be trained accurately and profoundly and to do the things that she has been trained to do with nothing but THOUGHT and PRESENCE OF MIND to back her up. And her thoughts are profound. Her ability to follow Commands is an illumination of the presence of her mind that entails the ongoing of her presence of being.

What mechanics of movement and the body are involved in the capability of following orders and Commands?

There is the movement of the head to ascertain a position that allows for the jaw to move open and to hold the food being presented to it by the handler. (The word "Handler" before this parenthesized section is the 47774th word. That is the number of Angels in a Trinity with time before and after the incident. That is what describes me! Interesting that it would say that! And as I was writing this sentence, another man from the Coffee Shop – a bicycle rider that I know – came over and started to say "Hi" to Paige. He had a new Golden Doodle that was 5 months old and playful, and Paige could smell him on the guy's runners. So funny! He is probably an Angel too!)

That last paragraph is an odd one. I don't think that you people who are readers of this book would accept that I am an Angel. Well, perhaps SOME of you would... but not all. There are some people that would think that it is an indication of craziness. But, if you believe in the Bible, or the Qur'an, which some people don't, but if you did, then you would have a reason to believe that the presence of Angels can become present throughout the existence of people. And some people can develop into Angels. And if you believe that, then you may also believe that the Soul of an Angel is an inhabitant of the body of Paige. And that is my belief... that Paige is the Soul and Spirit of an Angel!

And that is why here health is so profound! She has the capabilities to fight off diseases and illnesses that defies common comprehension! Thus, she upholds the highest realm of health there is!

BIOGRAPHY OF MITCHELL KRAUTANT

Krautant, Mitchell (2020). California, USA. IngramSpark.com

Mitchell Krautant is a genius who tested with a 142 IQ when he was in the USMC. He served in SOC Force

Recon there. He departed the Marines injured. Then he went to prison when he was innocent. They were highly illegal there and the prison staff gave him PTSD. He got sent to mind bending solitary confinement, which placed him under severe mental duress for 7 years after he was released.

When he was released, he went to college and was getting an A in calculus 2. But the mental trauma of solitary confinement overwhelmed him, so he dropped out of college and became homeless.

Mr. Krautant went homeless to the VA hospital and received no care there. He departed and was a victim of vehicular homicide. He died in the coma and was taken to the Hereafter by three of God's Angels. After he came back to life, he became an author.

He has written the *Cheetah on the Wing 1-4* books, *Movement to the Hereafter, Death and Life as a Victim of Vehicular Homicide,* and *The Elegant Lion Named George.*

There are even other books to follow!

www.mkrautant.com

Lightning Source UK Ltd.
Milton Keynes UK
UKHW021314081222
413609UK00021B/186